D1605806

Candy Cigarettes

A Small Town Memoir

Other works by Roger Bell:

Mythtakes	1984	Whizzyfig Press
Luke and the Wolf	1997	BS Poetry Society
Real Lives	1997	Black Moss Press
When The Devil Calls	2000	Black Moss Press
The Pissing Women Of Lafontaine	2005	Black Moss Press
You Tell Me	2009	Black Moss Press

As co-editor with John B. Lee:

Henry's Creature	2000	Black Moss Press

As editor:

Larger Than Life	2002	Black Moss Press

The Black Moss Press Settlements series gives writers a creative non-fiction forum for focusing on their roots, the "place" out of which their writing has emerged, and the study of the craft itself.

Books in the Settlements series include:

The Farm On The Hill He Calls Home, by John B. Lee – #1
Calling The Wild, by Roger Hilles – #2
Riding On A Magpie Riff, by Richard Stevenson – #3
When The Earth Was Flat, Raymond Fraser – #4
Left Hand Horses, John B. Lee – #5
The Gargoyle's Left Ear, by Susan McMaster – #6
When the Red Light Goes On, Get Off, by John Wing – #7
The Guthrie Road, by Rosemary Sullivan – #8
Alphabet Table, by Bruce Meyer – #9
Candy Cigarettes, by Roger Bell – #10

Candy Cigarettes

A Small Town Memoir

Roger Bell

2011

Library and Archives Canada Cataloguing in Publication

Bell, Roger, 1949-
Candy cigarettes / Roger Bell.

ISBN 978-0-88753-484-3

1. Bell, Roger, 1949- --Childhood and youth. 2. Poets, Canadian (English)--20th century--Biography. 3. Port Elgin (Ont.)--Biography. I. Title.

PS8553.E4564Z53 2011 C811'.54 C2011-900725-8

Black Moss Press is published at 2450 Byng Road, Windsor, Ontario, Canada N8W3E8. Black Moss books are distributed in Canada and the U.S. by LitDistco. All orders should be directed there.

Black Moss can be contacted on its website at www.blackmosspress.com.

Black Moss acknowledges the generous support for its publishing program from The Canada Council for the Arts and The Ontario Arts Council.

I dedicate this book to my parents, Bob Bell (1920-1996) and Bernice Rushton Bell (1927-1997); and to my brothers, Jim, John, and Chris. Boys will be boys, and Mom and Dad embraced that, offering a love-filled home where the four of us could become men while staying wide-eyed. May we never grow up.

ACKNOWLEDGEMENTS

I would like to thank the following:

Ed Rosner, Hank and Joan Smith, Ray and Mary Lou Fenton, Ken and Janet Dunlop – for adding to or correcting my sometimes incomplete, sometimes faulty recollections.

Marilyn Gear Pilling – for telling me I was on the right road and for helping me tighten "His Party."

Betsy Struthers – for helping me strengthen "Burn 3."

John B. Lee – for gamely reading the whole messy thing and improving the early and later bits.

The editing team of Anthony Balzer, Ian Clough, Sarah Colley, Gillian Cott, Emilia Danielewska, Alicia Di Giovanni, Beth Ann Hubbert, Erin Huitema, Josclyn Johnson, Kimberley Kovosi, Alicia Labbé, Paige MacKay, and Adam Willson for your unstinting energy, your wonderful ideas, your belief in the integrity of the work, your fresh eyes that saw what I was often unwilling or unable to recognize.

Marty Gervais – for continuing to have faith in me even when I have none.

Happy Days Diner, photographer Sandi Wheaton, and models, Aaron, Adam, and David Collins and Michael Schifanelli, for contributions towards the promotion of this book.

Bruce Meyer for providing the cover image.

The Ontario Arts Council – for financially supporting the creation of this work through their Writers' Reserve Fund.

"What Do You Know," "Age of Innocence," and "Burn 3" first appeared in *The Windsor Review*.

CONTENTS

AUTHOR'S NOTE

"I have used a factual background for most of my tales, and of actual people a blend of the true and the imagined. I myself cannot quite tell where one ends and the other begins."

Marjorie Kinnan Rawlings, *Cross Creek*

The memoir is a literary genre under scrutiny these days. Readers and critics demand, no, *need*, to know: Are these stories true? I answer: Yes, of course they are, but does it *really* matter? Aren't what happened and what I believe happened of equal weight?

Okay, I admit, in this book I may have *gently* fabricated or omitted or combined to protect someone; or, for literary effect, I may have *slightly* embellished or altered. But I assure you: this place, this time, these people existed, and they are as alive inside of me now as they were alive then. They are *so* real I can reach out and touch them. They are my ever-present past.

Warriors – Jim (left) and Roger in side yard on Market Street, circa 1957.

CHERRY BOMBS

It is the major explosives, the fat red cylinder called the Cannon Cracker and the squat dangerous Cherry Bomb that attract us most, because of what they can do. A Cannon Cracker strapped to the base of a six-foot sunflower can bring that baby to earth like a fir tee felled. A Cherry Bomb placed under a tin can is a huge impetus, propelling the container shudderingly high above the tree tops, where it hesitates, has a look around, before tumbling and toppling erratically back to earth.

One summer day, uptown, Glenn comes ambling along towards us, wearing shorts, a t-shirt, and, incongruously, tall red and black rubber boots on bare feet. There isn't a cloud between here and Michigan, the sun is relentless, those boots have to be sweat-hot. Oh temptation. Somebody, just to see what will happen, the only real reason we do most of the asinine things we do, lights the fuse of a Cannon Cracker and drops it inside Glenn's left boot. He becomes aware immediately, he hears and feels the sizzle, the imminence of disaster. At first he runs blindly, then hops, frantically trying to wedge that sweaty footwear off. He almost makes it, then *Whoomph!*, a hole the size of a fifty-cent piece opens like a lanced boil in the rubber sidewall. And he squeals and he curses and he rips the boot the rest of the way off. He rubs at a seared patch of skin, then, sheepishly smiles at us as we hold ourselves and rock and weep at the careless beauty of our accomplishment.

Another summer, outside the Dairy Bar, we're working avidly at triple-decker ice cream cones. Mine is orange-pineapple, my current favourite. Last year it was Rum n' Raisin. There are maybe six of us, lounging and licking in the shade of the awning, aimless in the afternoon. Somebody announces, "It's the Wizard of Oz," and sure enough, pop bottle glasses and freckles and loose grin, here he comes towards us. And it just unfolds, as if our brains are transistor radios all tuned to the same evil station. Orange-pineapple is the Wizard's favourite flavour too, I know, so I volunteer to sacrifice mine and someone quickly and smoothly shoves a Cannon Cracker all the way down through the bottom sphere of ice cream and into the cone, and someone else produces a lighter and somehow, defying probability, lights the fuse at just the right moment allowing me to turn fluidly to the just-arriving Wiz, holding the side of the cone with the sputtering fuse towards me, and say, "Hey Wiz, just got this, but gotta go, want the rest?"Like a trout hitting a lure, he accepts wordlessly, reaches out. You can almost hear his brain sigh. How can this be? How can he not hear the fuse? I have no idea, but the gods are with us. He moves the gift towards his mouth, his tongue begins to snake out for that first slurp, when *WHUPPPP!* He's covered, we're covered too, but we don't care, 'cause look at the Wiz: his glasses are opaque with slop, his hair is orange, his mouth is empty and gasping, his tongue hanging defeated, still clenched in his fist is a stub of cone; which he considers, then pops into his maw, chews, swallows. It doesn't get any better than this.

I'm roller skating on a buttery summer night, holding the hand of some tanned tourist girl, who may be named Pam, or maybe it is Pat, gliding along to *Sealed With A Kiss*. There is a tender breeze off the lake and we are synchronized, locked as we are in each other's gaze. She is wearing some perfume that simulates ripe cherries. My brain is Zenned on summer and a warm hand and our circling of the rink, the air is glowing all around us, is fuzzed like the tumbled Milky Way.

Out of the corner of my eye, from where my friends are sitting, something red and ugly and sizzling arcs into one of those forty-gallon drums they use for refuse, the forty gallon drum we are approaching in our counter-clockwise spin around this outdoor oval. I know what is about to happen, though I wish I didn't. I open my mouth to yell, "Cherry Bomb!" but all I get out is "Cher-" The remaining two syllables are swallowed up by a sonic wave that punches our chests and drives six-inch spikes into our ears. Her eyes are shocked moons. She's trembling, the whole earth is quaking. I try to tell her it's okay but I can't hear my own voice. So I grin deafly and stupidly at her, then at my friends, convulsed with laughter. I take her back to her cottage. Three days later, when she leaves to resume her life in Kitchener or whatever part of the outside world she inhabits, we say awkward, muted goodbyes. I never see her again, but I see those foolish friends daily. They can't stop talking about the look on that girl's face when the world erupted.

Still summer. Maybe it is always summer when our madness reigns - the heat, the idle hours. We're out in the back yard, Larry's back yard next door. We have fashioned a bazooka from a length of galvanized pipe. We have read way too many comics of Sgt. Fury and Sgt. Rock and his Howling Commandos. We want to be them, to lay waste. Into the arse end of the pipe we stuff a Cannon Cracker (we are blessed, we have a whole box of them) and into the mouth we tamp a ball bearing that someone liberated from the machine shop across the tracks.

Twenty feet away, Larry, wearing an ancient leather football helmet and felt hockey shoulder pads for protection, is leaning slightly forward with a two-inch thick, foot-wide plank propped against his back. The idea of our war game is to blast the bearing at the board, see if it will split the target. Someone else, possibly me, holds the bazooka on his shoulder and sights it. I have shredded Kleenex stuffed into my right ear, but I wear no goggles, since eyes are immune to explosions. My assistant, someone's younger brother, lights the fuse and *POW!* the silver sphere flies dead at the board and drives it, along with Larry, ahead two feet and face-first into the grass. He leaps back up, spitting turf from his teeth. "Cool," he shouts, "cool!" We retrieve the bearing, power up the bazooka, do it again and again. Everyone wants to shoot, everyone wants to hold the board.

Then, out the back door to hang up clothes comes my mom, just in time to see Larry lace a bearing at me, her eldest, protected only by the fragility of my helmet, a now disintegrating plank and utter ingenuousness. She slows, stops, mouth opening slowly so her cigarette dawdles and tumbles to the grass, processing, processing, then she drops the basket of laundry and charges at us, sputtering, "Are you all *crazy*? Are you all *crazy*? Are you all *crazy*?"

Yes, is the answer. Yes. Joyfully yes. We *are* all crazy. We are *all* crazy. *We are all crazy.*

WATER

For the forty weeks before you squirt into this world in the middle of a howling Bruce County blizzard, you float in amniotic bliss inside your mother. Your world is gentle heat and subtle tides, a slowing of time, a softened sense. So how fortuitous it is that you are taken home from that hospital to a small lake town nearby, and that the rhythms of your foetal life attune to the rhythms of that bigger body of water.

Wherever you go west in this town, you come to the lake. Far on the other side of what is really an inland sea, sits Michigan, but so distant it might well not exist. The water is the border of being. It may be white-crested and pounding in late October, frozen and spectral in deep winter, or warm and inviting in mid-July, when locals and tourists alike soothe their souls in its sandy shallows. It is always there, defining this town, and, by extension, you.

In summer you are always there, it seems. You learn to swim, learn not to fight the waves, not to butt heads with them, but to release over them; you learn to breathe and plunge your face back into the water and to let the air bubble back out slowly, slowly, until you must again turn your face back up and gulp. You learn the crawl, backstroke, sidestroke, the dead man's float, how to tread water, to stride jump, to dive. When you are very young your mother takes you down for your first swimming test. It is a pummelling rain, but a warm one, and your mother, after kissing you, hands you into the arms of Wally Heatherington, your instructor. You feel safe with Wally, do not whimper in protest as the two of you walk far out over your head to the raft. Wally sets you up there, retreats to where you can barely see him through the downpour. "Dive in and swim to me," he commands. You tuck your toes over the edge of the raft, crouch, extend your arms, your hands praying, and launch. The lake accepts you, you open your eyes, admire the ripples of the sandy bottom, then surface, pull towards him. "Good," he says with a pat on the head, "good. Now swim back to the raft, stride-jump in, keep the head up above the surface, and back-stroke to me." Water above, water below, you lose any sense of land. When you finally hit shore, your mom, waiting under an umbrella, vigorously towels you off. She hugs you, says she is proud of you. Wally tells her, "Bernice, this kid has the lake in him," and formally presents you with your badge.

Your dad is a country boy who learned to swim in the Saugeen River, and that made him strong in the water. After work he comes home and takes your brother and you to the lake. He calls it *washing off the day.* Your mom stays home finishing supper. After the three of you wade out, he drops to his knees and says, "Climb aboard." With both of you on his tanned back he begins a long smooth breast-stroke outwards, towards where the sun will set in three hours. Your legs trail lazily in the water. You are no burden to him, nor are you afraid of the depths below. He eventually stops, takes you back in at the same easy pace to where you can safely stand, then heads back out on his own this time, faster and more deliberately. When he returns, he always says, "That feels better." Some weight has been lifted. Back at home, you all wolf down the supper your mom piles on the table; it tastes wonderful, lake-enhanced. Your dad goes to tend his garden, your mom does up the dishes, you head out to play.

Your family passes long lazy Sundays at the lake, either at the crowded Town Beach or out at Goble's Grove. People drive their cars right down to the water. Sometimes they will wash them using buckets and soapy sponges. There are blankets spread everywhere, pails and shovels, coolers, people splayed out tanning or standing in the water up to their knees and gabbing. In town the water is full of heads that seem to bob like disembodied corks. Kids and seagulls shriek. The smell of fries in hot grease slides across the sand and makes your gut rumble. You can happily waste a day digging holes and filling them back in, piling pails full of wet sand up into turrets which fly seagull feather flags, digging moats around them and filling them, making drawbridges out of driftwood. You can swim and eat egg-salad sandwiches and swim more and eat vinegar-soaked fries. You can sit hypnotized by all that water and the way the sun loves it. You can suck on popsicles and when they are gone you can chew the stick. And you can swim, you need to swim, it would be a sin not to when all that water invites you so benignly. Until the day begins to lengthen towards evening and your skin looks like a prune's and your mom helps you gather up all your stuff and your dad helps you fill in any holes that remain, so that they won't surprise the bare feet of late night strollers, who walk the beach under the full moon, murmuring quietly as the offshore breeze stills the silvered lake, as wave-worn children tumble into fresh sheets and tumble downwards into dreamy depths.

Port Elgin Public School Grade 8 class, 1962,
Roger, lower left, arms crossed.

HIS VOICE

Mr. Moore is my favourite teacher. He is different, slightly distant, but admirable. We call him Sir because he wants us to, and because he has an element of knightliness to him. He reads to us daily, usually after lunch when we are weary from baseball and Red Rover. He is also a church minister and his mellifluous voice is an opiate transporting me from this fetid and very ordinary earth to a world of wonder. I imagine that when he preaches, it is rapturous. I imagine people faint. We are his lay congregation, both in Grade Five and again in Grade Seven.

When he looks at us with his deeply serious brown eyes, pauses, and begins,

> The road was a ribbon of moonlight
> over the purple moor...

I am lost, as lost as any soul in an opium den. I am a ghostly galleon tossed upon cloudy seas.

He lets someone bring in a cicada. We keep it in a jar on the ledge of one of those tall windows, where the sun will hit it. When the heat of the day begins to build, it commences its drone, like a single insect choir filling the room, from our dusty feet to the high ceilings. The hymn it sings is drowsy, calls sleep from the faraway hills into our souls.

He surprises us often. Once, Sir plays his musical saw for us. He plays it with all seriousness. We might be watching someone bow a Stradivarius. It is sweet, that sound, vaguely oriental, and it brings tears to my eyes that I am careful to hide.

One day he reads us a long sweet poem called "Fern Hill." He sounds wistful, as if the boy in the poem was someone he knew well. I try to imagine Sir old, then older, his dark hair and moustache going salt and pepper, then grey. I imagine him in a white bed in a sunny room. I hope that as he fails, someone with a palliative voice reads poetry to him. I hope he'll then sleep that eternal sleep peacefully, with a cicada singing to him from a far high hill, like the Balm of Gilead in his ear.

THE STRAP

He gets the strap more than anyone else in the school. He is strapped for farting, belching, blatantly scratching his privates, daydreaming, carving his name into the desktop, some days just for being him. He never does his homework, never answers questions. His nails and clothes are filthy, his teeth yellow. His knees touch the undersides of the desk because he has been kept back four times in Grade Four. He is waiting to be sixteen.

One day he takes me aside in the playground and shows me a well-thumbed black and white picture. In it, a naked woman sits in the lap of a naked man, both facing the camera. My ears go pink, but I try to act the sophisticate. "See that?" he asks, pointing at her thick bush. "See what?" I have no idea what I am supposed to be looking for. He points again, emphatically, to the base of the man's penis, the rest of it buried somewhere, I have no idea. I still think babies come out of women's navels. He looks at me, shakes his head, stalks off, having wasted his time.

He also, more successfully, once teaches me a song:

Last time I seen her
and I haven't seen her since
she was wackin' off my neighbour
through a barbed wire fence,
gonna tie my pecker to a tree, to a tree
gonna tie my pecker to a tree.

I quite like this ditty, though I have no clue what *wackin' off* is, and the only pecker I know is woodpecker. Sounds fun though, so I sing the song quite blithely the next day to a group of older men at the post office. Some wince, some snicker. Fortunately, a kinder one takes me aside and, much to my humiliation, explains it word for word to me, saying maybe I should just sing it to myself. I do, for weeks after.

Once, during a lesson on the explorers opening up North America, he is working away on a liquid centre golf ball with his big pocket knife. He solves the cover, then the tightly wound elastic. I watch fascinated. Radisson and Grosiliers can't compete. When he finally punctures the tough skin surrounding the core, some thick, black, acidic liquid bursts forth like pus from a cyst and splashes all over Sandra, who shrieks as if he's stabbed her. He gets strapped right in front of the whole class for that, twenty times on each hand. He takes it stoically, but when he gets back to his seat he sits heavily down, lays his head in his arms and begins to sob quietly. He cries himself to sleep. No one ever wakes him.

THE AMERICAN BOY

We are used to tourists in our town. They are mostly Canadian, from Toronto, Kitchener, Guelph, London. They arrive in cars loaded with inflatable beach toys and stay in cottages down near the lake, some for a week, some two, some the whole summer. They spend their lazy days digging in the sand and swimming and tanning, their post-prandial evenings strolling, playing games of chance at the beach carnivals, or watching the sun go blood red then purple as it boils down into the lake. They take photographs of one another with the immense inland sea as background. They scarf cones of fries drowned in vinegar or condiment-mounded foot-long hot dogs they buy at the beach. They feed the gulls and get upset when the gulls pay them back for their generosity by shitting on them. When they get bored of water and sun, or when it rains, as it often does in the middle two weeks of August, they gawk along the main street buying souvenir t-shirts, paperback books, jigsaw puzzles, postcards. These postcards they send back to the city so those left behind can be jealous. For two months each year they are a vital part of the town, but they aren't *part of* the town. They come, they laze, they buy, they leave; they may mingle but their presence doesn't take.

The American Boy is different. He comes for the whole summer, from Pittsburgh. We aren't exactly sure where it is but it's much further away than most tourists live. He isn't even a tourist, as such, his parents describe themselves as *summer residents*. It sounds official. It sounds rich, a bit snooty, a bit invasive, but almost within limits. They live in a place just a block over from us, a bungalow. Not a cottage, not on or near the beach. It is in a *permanent* part of the town the way the cottage area is not.

The American Boy says *soda* where we say *pop*, and when he speaks he does something funny with his vowels, but he is tanned and handsome, has an easy, disarming smile, and before we know it he is among us, a member of the roving group of kids. He plays scrub baseball with us, and street hockey (which we have made a year-round game in a vacant lot). He settles in so much that he tries out for and makes the baseball team; *of course*, we say, he *is* American, it *is* their game, he comes from the home of the champion Pirates, as if he merits playing by dint of that. Still, there are a few rumbles of discontent: he doesn't live here and should he be allowed to take a place away from a local kid? But that comes from adults, not us, and soon dies away.

What ingratiates him with us the most, what makes us eagerly anticipate his arrival in late June, is his wealth of baseball cards. We all collect them, trade them, spend hours sorting them and memorizing the stats on the back of each. We endlessly chew the brittle gum that accompanies them; our jaws ache and our teeth decay. The goal is to end up with a complete set, but for kids in our town, that is not possible. They are released in series, and there may be a sixth and seventh series, but only the first five ever make it to our area. Rumour has it that the States release all cards later to Canada and place an embargo on the final two series travelling outside their borders so that Canadian kids can't achieve the pinnacle. Until the American Boy comes to town, boxes full of all series, traders galore. The first day he arrives each June every collector in town is on his lawn trying to make a deal, waving paws full of cards in his direction, offering not just to trade but to *buy*, an unheard of transaction. I once, on the corner by the brush factory, parted with a hundred baseball cards not all of which were traders, to get my mitts on a Mickey Mantle rookie card. I'd never have bought it; that would cheapen the acquisition. But such is the desperation by the time the American Boy shows up with the last two series that buying, tawdry as it is, is countenanced.

We come to like the American Boy. It is easy to do so. He can go deep into the hole at shortstop to track down a sharply hit grounder, he can turn a double play with little effort. He can and will help you fill out your Cleveland Indians or New York Yankees roster. If he hasn't the card you need he'll gladly write a friend back in Pittsburgh and a week later it will arrive in the mail. He comes to feel like a local. His bicycle is battered, missing a couple of spokes, no better than ours. His ball glove, as does mine, has a shoelace holding the fingers together since the original leather thong rotted and snapped. He has no more money to spend on ice cream or firecrackers than the town boys. When the group assembles, he is there unobtrusively, and when we finally head home at dark, begrudging the darkness its allotted hours, he is one of the last to leave.

So it is amazing how this assimilation is so easily undone, all in one day, all in one frenetic outburst. We are playing summer hockey in the lot beside my house. We have two homemade nets there, two by fours, nails and burlap. We have worn the grass down to hard dirt with our ceaseless to-and-froing. We have a barrel of sticks that is permanently there, a couple of goalie sticks, a sponge ball maybe a bit ratty but still round enough to roll true. There are maybe twenty of us, divided into two teams; each team has five players and a goalie on the field. The others watch, await their chance to leap into the fray, replace a gasping teammate. The American Boy is, of course, there. He does something with the ball, or to someone, I am not really sure, it's so fast, part of the action. I was going for a pass and had my back to them. He is standing toe to toe with the other guy. Play has been suspended, the ball allowed to roll red white and blue off to the side. They are arguing about what the American Boy did, whether or not it's allowed. And the American Boy says, and as he says it you can sense a permanent shift, "Back in Pittsburgh, we do it all the time." And there are suddenly nineteen of us and one of him, and he looks small and vulnerable and horribly alone. The guy he has been arguing with says with a sneer, "Well why don't you just trot right back to Pittsburgh and play then?" And knocks the stick from his hands. Gives him a shove backwards, towards Pittsburgh. And someone else yells out, maybe trying to be funny but instead inflaming things, "Yankee, go home!" Someone else picks up this refrain, then we are all saying it, and the American Boy is standing in the middle of us all by himself crying, his fists balled up. He starts for home, still snivelling, looking back longingly over his shoulder. He'd like to fight, defend his honour, but he sees the odds and he knows he is again, now irredeemably, a foreigner, he has crossed some line. There is silence for a few seconds but before we can think too deeply about what we have just done, or whether it even merits reflecting upon, someone has taken his place and the ball is again rolling; the game continues as if it had never stopped.

IN THE CORNER

I'm facing a stack of books. Old, mouldy, dusty. I fight the urge to sneeze. I have behind my back, as instructed, one hand clasping the other "where they can't get grabby." David is somewhere in the other corner; I wonder if he is as miserable as I am, so I swing my shoulders to look. "Get that head back around, mister!" I do, quickly, my heart pounding. I am afraid of the teacher, startled by her sharp voice, her imperiousness. I am new to Kindergarten, new to its restrictions. I don't want to learn. I don't need to. I can already count to 100, I can already read, my mom taught me.

Next year we will go to Grade One in the big school down from my grandparents. All day! I don't care to do that either. I already feel infringed upon losing my mornings. By the time I get home it's lunch, then a half hour of radio when I listen to Mr. Bing, who tells wonderful stories, then at the end says, "Time for your nap, boys and girls, now *ssssscccccoooooot!*" And I jump up and run upstairs to bed and when I wake up the day is almost gone. My mother says I should be happy going to school, that as you grow up you must do that, you must give things up. I see no advantage in growing up.

I feel hard done by. My friend Janice was sitting building a wall of words with blocks, wooden ones that had a letter carved into each side. I left my table to go over and ask her to come play at my table, but before I could, Mrs. Lesperance demanded I go back to my seat. "Now!" And she didn't say please. "I will in a minute," I replied. It took her a lot less than a minute to zip over, lift me up and plunk me back down in my chair. She returned to working some plasticine with other kids. Janice was looking at me, making that *What?* sign with her hands turned out, palms up. I went back to her table; Mrs. Lesperance was distracted. "Come play at my table," I invited Janice. "She's staying here," piped up David, who sat with her.

Janice looked uncertain. "She's my girlfriend," I told David. He stood up. "No. She is mine," he retorted. I took her by the arm, tried to lift her from her seat. David latched onto her other arm, and a fierce tug of war for the boyfriendhood of Janice began. "You're hurting me," she wailed, but David and I were oblivious to her pain, staring hard at each other, yanking at her. A chair went over, blocks scattered off the table. Then Mrs. Lesperance was upon us. "Let her go," she commanded through clenched teeth, but neither of us would cede the territory of Janice. I felt the teacher's fingers dig into my wrists and jerk my hands from my friend's arm, which bore my red fingerprints. She tugged David loose from the other arm. She was breathing hard, her eyes little more than slits. Janice was wailing, rubbing at her wrists, wiping snot from her upper lip. Two other girls came up, hugged her, glared at David and me, started picking up the dumped blocks and placing them back on the table. Mrs. Lesperance dragged us away from the others. She leaned down into our faces. "Exactly what was that all about?" I told her Janice was my girlfriend; I told her I loved Janice. "I love her more," said David. The woman shook her head in disbelief. "If you two think that is how to show love, dislocating the poor girl's arms, you're badly mistaken. Get in opposite corners." We both hesitated. "Now! You're just lucky I'm not giving you the strap."

So here I am, staring at the intersection of two walls, bored silly, getting stiff from standing still. I discover that if I slide my eyes to the right I can see Janice. She isn't crying anymore; in fact, she is laughing away with the girl who has replaced David at the table. The wall of words is growing again. She happens to look up, sees my glance, whispers something to her tablemate, who looks up, scowls at me, then they both stick out their tongues at me and titter, smug in their girlness. I close my eyes and start counting off the seconds until we get to go home. I will have tomato soup with soda crackers broken up into it; I will have celery stalks with Cheez Whiz slathered into the wide Us; I will have Pantry cookies with milk and I will break the cookies in two and dip them until they get soggy then I will suck them in noisily. After lunch I will curl up beside the radio and hope Mr. Bing plays the story of Peter and the Wolf, the one where the musical instruments play the characters. When he finishes I will *sssscccoooooot* at his behest up to bed and when I wake I will run out into the day and appreciate it. The day will have no girls and it will have no corners.

Kindergarten class, Port Elgin Legion Hall, 1953-54,
Roger, 3rd row centre, striped shirt, curly hair.

BURN

1

The flames licking my bare legs and spreading more rapidly than I thought possible have made me realize why my father, when he employs me, gives me simple tasks, seemingly foolproof ones. How I could have let this happen I do not know; it makes me want to stop and weep, but I don't have time if I am to prevent the whole block from going up in smoke.

He dropped me off at his lot across from the arena, the one with the big barn where he stores all his lumber and tools, and told me to rake up last fall's leaves and burn them. Then I was to cut the grass. He'd come back and get me in a few hours. He had faith that I could do all this without screwing up. He dropped me off and turned me loose with a rake and some matches; he wants to put money in my pocket and give me a sense of accomplishment.

Now here I am and here this runaway fire is and how simple it should have been and how complicated it's become. I feel like Sinbad the Sailor facing a baby roc with his tiny sword. Look what's hatched out of this egg! I raked and raked, easy because the leaves were dry and the breeze was firm from the south; I knew to rake with the wind, knew how to sweep with the rake, like brooming, so the leaves were picked up and flew a few feet. Faster, more efficient. I'd be done before I knew it, maybe wander down to the pool hall, shoot a couple games of Boston, maybe make some money that way too. When I got half the lot done, I paused, took a long, satisfying slug of icy water from my thermos, surveyed the situation. I had a large wave of leaves the whole width of the lot. I had a firebreak three feet wide ahead of it. I'd burn those, then rake and burn the rest. Organized. Competent. Forward thinking. Organized, yes; the others vapourized the moment I lit the heaped leaves. The wind picked up, not much, but enough; within seconds, a few flaming leaves were borne aloft and deposited further up in the unraked grass.

Though I want to puke, I also admire the physics of the show, the ardour of the fire, how it moves faster than I can. Though I've grabbed a round-nosed shovel from my dad's shed and am running frantically along slamming it down hard, every one of my strokes that smothers one small clump sees a new clump eagerly ignite somewhere near. I'm so sweat-soaked and brain-addled, I think maybe I could extinguish this by simply rolling in it. Maybe I should piss on it. Maybe I should just drop the shovel, run far, far away before my dad gets back and boots me in the ass. I look up from where I flail uselessly and see that I am so far up shit creek all the paddles in the world won't bail me out: the flames are now perilously close to the storage barn, the one full of wood, power tools, scaffold. Oh Jesus, save me. And in all that dry heat, I find time for tears.

And Jesus does in fact save me, in the form of the man who lives on one side of my dad's lot and the woman who lives on the other. He runs out from nowhere, in his undershirt, his suspenders slung down over his pants, and he is trailing a hundred feet of garden hose from whose brass nozzle erupts salvation. And she, clad in apron and housedress, is everywhere with a broom, slapping savagely and persistently at recalcitrant flaring piles as if she does this every day between baking and ironing. Among the three of us, we tame the beast, put it out just before it reaches the shed and its valuable contents.

We are standing, breathing hard, allowing ourselves to smile weakly, looking at the last wisps of smoke, when my dad drives up. He alights from his van and looks quizzically towards me. The neighbour man steps right up to him, forms a breakwater, assures him it *wasn't* my fault, that the wind *did* suddenly pick up just as I lit the piles. I want to hug him. The neighbour woman squeezes my arm reassuringly and goes back to whatever our adventure pulled her from; the man begins to slowly recoil the hose towards his house. I extinguish a few remaining hot spots, though there is little worry now; nothing much remains that is combustible.

"Guess you don't need to worry about the grass now." My dad pauses, allows himself a chuckle. My mouth's too dry to laugh, my throat too tight. "I thought maybe you'd use the mower on it though, not incinerate it. Wanting to save time and gasoline, were you?" He's trying to get me to laugh, but there is nothing left in me right now. I hang my head and climb up into the van's passenger seat. Dad climbs in, turns it on, we pull slowly out. All the way home I imagine he must be wondering what it is in life exactly that I'm cut out for. Damned if I know either. When we get home, he reaches into his pocket, pulls out a wad of cash, pays me, my mouth hanging open; I did not expect it, but I should have, it's the kind of man he is. I got the job done, if somewhat unorthodoxly. And he doesn't tell my mom; I'm grateful for that, though I know she'll hear soon; this town is too small. My foul-up will be all over by tonight. I'll be the butt of jokes for days.

I take a shower, put on fresh clothes, decide to head up to the pool hall. Just as I go out the front door, two of my friends ride up on their bikes. They look at each other, nod, one says, "One. Two. Three." and in unison, they sing the opening to the Johnny Cash song: "I fell into a burning ring of fire..." Then they nearly piss their pants laughing. I can't help myself, I join in. I get on my bike, we ride up to my dad's lot, stand there staring in amazement at the blackened grass and the unscathed barn. One of them turns to me and asks, in admiration, "How *do* you do it?" The same question my dad would no doubt like to ask me. A question for which there is no answer. From the middle of the property, a single unburned maple leaf, a tiny miracle, lifts on a breath of air and climbs until it escapes the mercilessness of gravity.

COOL 1

As I walk uptown to get coffee cake at Ella Bolander's bakery, I pass by Henry's Men's Clothing. And stop. In the window he has fitted on a mannequin flared green tweed herringbone pants and a paisley patterned shirt to match. My heart flips! Carnaby Street comes to this tiny town, I think, and forgetting the coffee cake, march right in.

Henry is sitting at his desk in the little office at the back, smoking. I like Henry. He has a moustache, is a dapper dresser. I think he fits the word debonair. He stands up when he sees me, sets the cigarette carefully in an ashtray, steps out between the maroon curtains that give his office some privacy. I tell him what I am interested in, he smiles, nods, goes in search of a pair of the pants and a shirt in my size. "You'll want this too," he says, handing me a wide belt with a huge ornate buckle. When I come out of the change room, stand in front of the mirror, I can't stop smiling. I am a Mod, straight off TV, with my high collar and big stiff cuffs, with my trendy flares. I already have Beatle boots, so now I am complete.

I have Henry cut the tags off, put my old clothes in a bag, and I wear my outfit home. "Where's the coffee cake?" is all my mother demands when I walk in the door. Crap, I'll have to go back. But that's not so bad, I get the chance to show off all the way uptown. "Forgot," I say, "but I'll go back. Mom, what do you think of this?" She glances over from where she is setting the dining room table. "Nice," she says distractedly, goes back to folding napkins and setting out cutlery. She's having people for dinner and can't focus on me. I need someone to. So I go next door where Larry and four of his friends who are starting a band are flailing away at their craft. His mom is sitting out in a lawn chair, her eyes half-shut, her face towards the sun. She has her glasses in her hand and I can see a red mark across the bridge of her nose where they fit too tightly. "Such bloody noise," she says, jerks her thumb towards the house. "I couldn't stand it any longer, I had to get out from the midst of that. I hope they get better. Soon." It isn't noise to me. Music has more and more become like breathing, and I go eagerly in, occupy a far corner, listen to a ragged version of Talahassee Lassie. They stop, there is much gesticulation, and a heated discussion of how the drums and bass are out of synch. Larry, scowling, turns towards me, and as he does, his face lights up. "Cool!" he yells, "Very cool." He rushes over to finger the collar, exclaim over the big flares. "You are so Mod, Roger." The others, less overtly, also admire my gear. He and his band-mates are three years older. I want their approbation. They are almost a band, and that is the epitome of cool. If someone cool says I'm cool, I am.

I listen some more, then I leave, head for Ella's, do a peacock walkabout, singing a personalized version of the Manfredd Mann song: "Here I am just a-walkin' down the street, singin' doo wah diddy diddy dum diddy doo." Coming home, my flares swish and the coffee cake is fragrant, still warm inside its paper bag. I anticipate how sweet that first slice will taste.

SHAME

We spend a lot of our time in the summer evenings just cruising around. *Cruising* is such a euphonic word, that lazy z sound perfect for the langourousness of what we do. No destination in mind, heedlessly eating up the evening - down to the lake, out the North Shore, turn around, back along the public beach, up the hill to the main light, right on the main street out past the tobacco fields to the edge of town, u-turn, back north along the main street, out past the tobacco fields there, turn around, back down to the lake. The radio is always turned to CKLW in Windsor. Sometimes we sing along, we know every word to every song. Sometimes not, we listen only, lost in motion. The windows are always down, our arms hanging out against the cool metal doors; the night is always liquid.

Once darkness falls, we are granted immunity and can do other things from the anonymous safety of the moving car. Sometimes we moon people we know, sometimes we moon strangers, tourists out strolling, taking the air. There is so-and-so with his new summer girlfriend, walking hand in hand under the big spreading maples and the spangle of stars and the swollen love-struck moon above that. The driver spots them, alerts us, slows, the passenger side occupants unbuckle, drop drawers, kneel on the seats, shove glowing white bare asses out the windows. We can hear the sharp intake of breath from the scandalized girl, see her stop and point; we can see so-and-so half recognize us, or the car, realize that his perfect date has just been soiled, his chances with this girl diminished if not ruined, we can see him hang his head. The car erupts with sadistic laughter, and the driver speeds us away.

Sometimes we will slow alongside a group of girls we don't know, ask them their names, where they're from, how long they're staying, whether they want to get in and cruise with us. *Cruise* is less euphonic here, it takes on a charge, a muscularity, a barely suppressed animalism. Sometimes we will stop, pull over, and the braver girls come right to the car, lean down and rest their arms on the metal and look in at us, demonstrate that they see through us, that we are talkers, not doers. They never accept. But one night, one leans right in my window; I smell alcohol on her breath, see that she is older than I. I notice the fine dark hairs on her arm on the window sill, the crush of her breasts against the door, the deep magenta of her lipstick. She says nothing, examines me, I feel her eyes inside me. I think my heart will break out of my chest. Then. She reaches in, hooks her arm around my head, pulls me half out the window and kisses me, her tongue playing with mine, her mouth soft and hard at the same time, her hand gripping the back of my head as if she'll pull my face through hers, her eyes wide and boring deeper than I care to be explored. The inside of my head clangs. Then, no warning, she stops and turns and walks to her friends on the sidewalk. Nobody in the car says a word. None of the girls says a word. Suddenly our driver tips his head back and howls like a wolf, the other guys join in, the girls on the sidewalk too, and our driver laughs aloud, steps on the gas, squeals onto the asphalt, the tires smoking and protesting, the car hurtling into the stunned night. When I go home, I cannot sleep. My heart won't quit pounding. I want to see her again but know I won't; I can't even remember what she looked like.

A week later, everything about cruising changes. We see Sue walking by herself. Rumour is (and who ever questions rumours?) that Sue serviced the whole Senior Boys' basketball team one night at a party last fall. I am such a smart-ass, so clever, so good with words, I will play upon her name, I am protected by darkness and movement and moral superiority. I lean out the window and do my best pig-calling. *Sooey,* and again, elongated for hurtful effect, *Sooooooooooey.* Then we drive off, cackling. We reach the lake, turn around, back up that same street, eager for more, and there she is, still walking, unwavering. We slow. My mouth opens but she pre-empts me, spits out, *I know that's you, Roger Bell, I know that's you.* I slump, I try to hide, my face is on fire, I must glow in the night so that everyone can see my culpability. I ask to be let out at the main street. I wonder what has happened to me, I wonder who I am become. I wonder, if I can force myself to look in a mirror, will I even recognize the boy who looks back? And will I want to?

Roger on tractor in front of Charlie Schell's garage, circa 1950.

HIS PARTY

"I don't want to go." My mother sets down the brush she's been tugging through my curly hair, picks up a wet washcloth and scrubs my face vigorously. She is clamped down on her cigarette, her face wreathed in smoke, and frowning, the way she does when I do not accede to her wishes. "You're going." "But nobody else will be." "Of course they will; and even if they don't, *you* are going, and you will *like* it." She lifts me off the counter, straightens my bow tie, smoothes my English Sweater. My English Sweater really is from England. My brother has an identical one. They are light brown with horizontal green, blue and red lines, some wider, some narrower. They zip up the front. They are hand-knit from what must be the roughest itchiest wool in the whole world, from barbed-wire sheep that don't say *baa* but say *baw*, and came as gifts from the wealthy family of my mother's English war bride sister-in-law. So we will wear them come hell or high water, says my mother. She shouldn't say hell; my grampa did and my gramma gave him a tongue-lashing. Our

English Sweaters are our best clothes, and we wear them in all weather if the occasion demands some formality.

Today is such an occasion. I have been invited to the birthday party of a boy in my class. He comes from a poor family. He and his siblings smell funny and they are fat. My mom says they are fat because all they eat is potatoes, which are cheap. They can't afford meat. They do the best they can with what they have, she says. My mother says they aren't poor, they've had bad luck, that's all. They were both in the war and served their country proudly and now their luck has turned bad and that is no reason to reject them. The people that do are trash. The way she says *trash* makes me afraid she will bite through her cigarette and swallow the unlit part and have to go to the hospital.

She is thorough with her inspection of me, and is more gentle. She puts her cigarette aside, hands me the brightly wrapped present, leans down to take my face in her hands, kisses me, and walks me to the door. "Have fun." And I find myself walking towards the afternoon. It is a gorgeous spring Saturday. I want to be out on my bike, not itching and hot, not prissied to death, not on my way to a party of someone I don't really like or even know. He's in my class, that's all, not enough to make me want to go to his party. I'm afraid, too. What is a house of poor people like? Is it dangerous? Will it fall down, like the old witch's house over on Market St. is falling down? Will it smell, as the boy smells at school when he's been playing in the rain at recess and the heaters are on? Will there be potato peels piled everywhere?

The house is insul-bricked and leans a bit. It has lilac bushes that have run a bit wild so that you can't really go in the front door, you have to go around to the side, through a woodshed with wood stacked along one wall, where it feels damp and spidery. I raise my hand to knock, pull it back down, feel sweaty and itchy, take a deeper breath, reach back up and before I can touch the door with my knuckles it is pulled open, as if someone has been watching my approach, and there is his mother, big and red-faced and frizzy-haired, wearing a dress and an apron. "Come in," she says, "come in," and into their kitchen I go. The whole family is there, his two brothers and his two sisters, all dressed up. There are balloons hanging from a strip of flypaper that has more flies than paper showing but the rest of the room looks scrubbed clean. "Welcome, "says his father, who has a paunch and is wearing suspenders so that the top of his pants sits well below his belly, and who bends down to shake my hand. I feel strange: shaking hands is an adult thing, something my dad and his friends do, something formal, but no one has ever shaken mine before. His handshake is doughy and wet.

"The table isn't quite ready," says his mom, "and none of the other boys are here yet, so why don't you boys go out and play?" I don't say anything, just hold out the present my mom spent so much time wrapping. My mom is a good wrapper; things must be even, properly folded. The ribbon must be curled just so. She says she learned it when she worked in the clothing store at Christmas. His mom takes it from me with a huge smile and places it upon the sideboard beside the cake, which is white, the frosting covered in coconut. It looks like winter, but it is hot enough in the kitchen to be full summer.

We go back out through the woodshed. "Want to play catch?" he asks. I like catch, I play it with my dad after he is done work, or with my brother, or my grampa, so I say sure; maybe this day will be okay after all. He picks up a sponge ball off the ground, a ball so old that most of the red, white and blue stripes are barely visible. "Do you have gloves?" I ask. He shakes his head. My brother and I have gloves, fawn coloured ones, brand new, that we got last week because baseball season has started and we will be playing each week at Lakeview Park. My dad took us up to

Tupling's Sports and Hardware and let us pick them out. He told us they were late birthday gifts or early Christmas ones, whichever sounded best to us. I know we don't have much money, that these gloves cost a lot, that our father loves us, that he loves baseball. When I watch him play he is elegant and lean, he moves gracefully across the outfield for his team, the Monarchs. I know that it is important to him that we have these gloves. They smell of new leather; I can sit for hours in the porch just listening to a Yankees game on the radio and sniffing my glove and working in the pocket. The birthday boy tosses me his ball; it is heavy, soaked. It has been outside in the grass for ages, I think. It has what looks like a bite out of one side. Because of the bite it wobbles, too. But we develop a game, high toss, low toss, tricky grounders. And for a repeated while, time moves easily.

Nobody else comes. His dad finally shows up to fetch us. His mom gives him a hug; he knows I am it, he looks as if he may cry. "It's time for lunch," she says bravely. "I don't know why none of the other boys are here. I specifically said noon on the invitations. And past noon it is." She shakes her finger at the wall clock as if the poor attendance is the clock's fault. "We shall make a party of it anyway." His father applauds. I think his fingers look like chubby breakfast sausages slapping together. We move to the table, which is set for fourteen. "You sit here," they tell me, "beside the birthday boy." Someone pulls the chair out for me and as I sit, a long, wet, farting noise escapes from under my bum. I blush loudly, and the others all howl, but I don't laugh. My sweater feels like it is knit from nettles. How did that fart happen? He reaches under me and pulls out a little rubber bladder with a neck: a whoopee cushion. They are still laughing wildly, the whole family. I can see their teeth, and tears course down their faces, all puffy, all red and misshapen. Now I want to cry, I feel like a freak in a carnival, my whole face is aching from the false fart shame, and the mother recognizes that and calms the others. Palm down, she pats the air in front of her. "Come now," she says," come now, time to serve our guest." The merriment dies slowly, eyes are wiped and noses blown, and a huge platter of sandwiches, egg and salmon and peanut butter and banana, all with the crusts cut off and sectioned into triangles and circles, is shoved at me. Salmon, I think, is very expensive. How can they afford this? I thought we'd be having potatoes. I take one of each kind and we eat. The sandwiches are good, and I ask for more. "Eat up," says his dad, "eat up. You're eating for seven." He laughs at his own joke, but no one else does. I sneak a sideways glance at the birthday boy, who is chewing blankly, his big brown eyes vacant. I wonder where those other six boys are. There is another platter of sandwich untouched on the sideboard; I can't help but think all that expensive salmon wasted.

The cake follows, dry and crumbly, not as good as the sandwiches. My mother makes the best cakes; she makes them for bake sales and beach carnivals; she makes angel food cakes with Richmond frosting, all swirls. All the tourists try to win them at the carnival bake table. I wonder what she would say about this white thing I'm gamely trying to shovel down by mixing it with mouthfuls of raspberry Kool Aid. I am saved from a second piece by presents, two of them. Mine, which is opened first, is a model ship, a destroyer, about which there is much oohing and ahhing, and the father breaks into a big smile. "That is the very ship I served on in the war," he announces. "However did you know?" "I didn't," I say, not wanting to add that the reason I bought it was it was the cheapest I could find. He holds up the box at all angles to the ceiling, as if he has X-ray vision and can see the boat to be completed inside. As if he can see himself on the deck of it in rolling seas, looking for U-boats. Then the family present, a new sponge ball and a small bat. "You boys take it out and play. Give it a try," says his mom, "we girls and Dad will clean up."

We try, we really do, but Scrub with only one fielder wears out quickly. It is like a smile with almost no teeth. There is too much room, as there was too much room at the table. This game was planned for nine boys, but the four of us do our best. We decide to do without the catcher, but then the batter gets nasty with the pitcher who can't find the plate and soon we give up.

When I get home, my mom asks me all about it. I don't get past the part where no one else showed. I want to tell her about my surprise at salmon, and how her cakes are the world's best, but she is chewing furiously on her cigarette and interrogating me about the names of the boys who didn't come. One lives just three blocks away, and with me in tow my mother strides over there, practically pulling my arm off. The boy, who is tall for his age and freckled, is out front riding aimless circles on his bike, practising doing it with no hands. My mother glares at him then raps sharply on the front door. His mother, wiping her hands on a dish rag, opens it, smiles, starts to say something small-town, but my mother doesn't let her. She spits out the story of the birthday party and how only I showed, how her son was invited but... The other mother looks slightly guilty, says, almost apologetically, "Well, I'm sorry, but no way I'm sending my son over there. Their kids smell, the parents smell, and neither works. Not the type of people I want to associate with. I'm afraid my son might *catch something* there." It is those two words that set my already smouldering mother alight. "You are trash," says my mother "and worse still, you are a snob. Don't forget, I knew you when your family didn't have a pot to piss in." The towel drops from the woman's hand and her mouth falls open. "C'mon," Mom says to me, "let's go home before we... *catch something*."

With that Mom hoists me up, hugs me hard, and we head home. I love my mother's fierceness. I'm not quite sure what she just did, but it somehow feels good. When we get home, she strips my English Sweater off me, kisses me, says what a good boy I was to go to the party. I tell her that she is the best cake maker, and all about the dry birthday one that I ate anyway, to be polite. "Come with me," she says, "I've been baking while you were away." On the counter are three angel cakes, ready for that night's beach carnival. "Choose," she says. "Huh?" "Choose your birthday cake." "But it's not my birthday." "Yes, it is; it's every good boy's birthday today. Choose." I select the chocolate. She seats me at the table and brings me a huge slab with a glass of icy milk, then when I am done, another slice. I am stuffed. I go over and try to hug her where she is occupied separating a dozen yolks from their whites. "Not now," she says, then adds, to avoid seeming ungrateful, "I don't have much time to get this third cake done, so go outside and play."

I get my new glove and my sponge ball. I go to the north side of the house, the side with the least windows and the most wall, begin mindlessly hurling the ball against the siding and catching it when it bounces back. This is the perfect game for one, I realize. I am mesmerized by the blue, white and red sphere, the way it spins back in a blur each time, directly into the pocket of my glove. Everything eventually falls into place, like my father loping gracefully in the freshly cut grass of the outfield and hauling in a high fly ball, like my mother happy in her kitchen, busily whipping those yolks into an airy froth and humming.

Roger's first hockey stick, Christmas circa 1952.

THE SPANISH LESSON

It is my turn to read and I stand up confidently. Today's story is about a boy living in Mexico. I start: "Juan... (I pronounce it *Wan*. How I know to do this is a mystery.)... Juan had a burro that he took to town each day..." She stops me, holds her hand palm out at me, like a traffic cop. "What did you just say?" I am puzzled, I made no mistakes, I'm sure, so I repeat, "Juan had a burro that he took to town each day..." She interrupts, "That's *Jew-ann.*" She leans into each syllable, elongating it. "Pardon?" "*Jew-ann.*" She repeats it slowly and patiently, as if I am simple. "No," I say, "no, it's *Wan.*" The room is very quiet, pregnant with expectation. No one questions this teacher. She is fierce, she is old. I once saw her pick up Whitey by the front of the shirt so forcefully that she tore it half off him, then shake him so hard his eyes rattled. It was February 14. He had given her one of those phony Valentine cards that said on the front, "You look like a million bucks," but when you turned it over added "all green and wrinkled." "No" she repeats, this time through clenched teeth, "no, it's *Jew-ann*, and you will read it as such. Start now, please." "*Wan*" is barely out of my mouth before she's out from behind her desk and beside me. I am lifted off my feet and shoved face-first into a corner of the room full of old books that smell of mildew and neglect. And there I stand until reading period finishes, my ears burning, my bladder threatening to let go. Saying over and over in my head, "Wan Wan Wan" and imagining a small brown-skinned Mexican boy of my age, sweating in the harsh light as he drags a stubborn old burro, all green and wrinkled, into town each day.

CENTRIFUGAL FORCE

I plant my right elbow onto the desktop, settle my head into the palm of my hand, look left out the tall open windows into the perfect late September morning. The day is generously warm and sunbathed, the sky high and flawlessly blue above the maples, which are beginning to surrender their green to inevitable autumn. It's a day almost too good for this waning time of year, its beauty made more profound by its finiteness.

The physics lesson is a barely intrusive murmur. Chicky, a small lean bald man with a gentle voice, is up at the blackboard patiently explaining why a baseball curves and dips. I adore baseball. I can sit and watch a game unfold on a long and languid afternoon and not care if it ever ends. I should listen to what he has to impart about seams and air pressure and rotation, but explaining why a thrown ball does what it does borders on heresy. Let Whitey Ford and Jim Kaat and Mudcat Grant just do what they do. Keep it in the realm of magic. Besides, this is Fall Fair Friday, more conducive to dreaming than it is to learning. In another five minutes it will be noon and an afternoon off in the Fairgrounds is beckoning.

Half-way between the main street and the water are the big gates into the Fairgrounds, also called Lakeview Park, a huge square with mature maples around its perimeter and inside that, a wide dirt track a quarter mile long. Later in the day the trotters and pacers will thunder around it. For now it is full of strollers and ditherers. I always turn right at the gates and immediately head to the Palace, a two-storied wooden building that once must have been magnificent, almost palatial, but is now starting to weather and sag. I take the double-wide staircase to the second floor two steps at a time, looking for my grandmother somewhere among the quilts and flowers. She will be, as every year, competing against Mrs. Rae, her arch-rival. If in her mind the judges have shown good sense, my gramma's vases will be red-ribboned, she'll be in an effusive mood, hug me, give me a couple of dollars to spend *foolishly,* tell me, "Get out of this musty old barn and away from these musty old girls, find your friends and have fun." I take her money and her advice and head downstairs, but I can't leave without seeing the pies: plump apple, fluffy lemon meringue beginning to weep in the heat, carefully latticed cherry and raisin. Each missing a thin wedge, defiled out of the need for judging. I stand drooling, imagining the sweet tiny individual explosions in my mouth. Suddenly ravenous, I head for the food stand where my friends have gathered. The Throat has already absorbed two loaded foot-longs and a slab of maple fudge. He is gargling down a cherry shake that he will follow with a Coke and fries. He isn't called the Throat for nothing.

Aimless and late summer sun-struck, we wander, a group in flux. A trio slides off into the midway, a going-steady couple wanders off to find a private necking spot near the Town Pond below the hill, the rest continue on to be joined by several fresh from the Palace. We are a school of lazy fish in a warm river of afternoon. We swim into livestock. The girls turn red and gabble among themselves at the sight of a Clydesdale stallion with a huge glistening erection, at a ram energetically covering a ewe, at the burden-heavy balls of a Black Angus bull that grazes misleadingly placid, tethered by a nose ring. The rich smell of shit is everywhere. Men and women, their faces scrubbed raw by the outdoor life, lean against fences or sit on bales of hay. The odd bored kid chews on straw. A group of men plays cards boisterously, taking sips of something strong and dark in paper cups. A corresponding group of women sits crocheting at a nearby table, where they offer farm-fresh eggs in large corrugated flats, home baking like Chelsea Buns and tea biscuits, and last spring's maple syrup.

We drift next to the centre of the park, the main ball diamond, climb up into the bleachers where we sprawl and watch a bunch of elementary school students playing softball. They aren't very good, the bats are too big for them. We yawn, talk music, lie back on the wooden seats and soak up the heat. Then someone suggests more food, so back we go to the booth. I buy a candy floss for a girl I like from the next town; she has dark hair and big, serious eyes, she can make my heart stop in the hall at school just by saying hi. She plucks off an airy waft of the floss; I open my mouth, begging, she puts it on my tongue. I close my lips, she smiles, oh wow, she lets me suck the pink sugar from her fingers. I close my eyes. When I open them, she is delicately plucking gobs of floss off the paper cone and stuffing them in her mouth. Meanwhile the Throat continues his rampage, downs a burger with cheese and bacon, a candy apple, a ginger ale, a Crispy Crunch.

As the day begins to shine even more brightly and lengthens into shadows which surge ahead of our growing group, I find myself hand-in-hand with the dark-haired girl. We visit and re-visit everything inside the grounds. The day cools slightly but we do not. We are making the most of an afternoon that feels illicit. As we trail the pack, the girl whose hand I am holding perhaps too tightly, afraid she will evaporate, jerks me to a stop. She looks into my face with her serious grey eyes, pulls me behind a horse trailer and places her hand behind my head, draws my face down to hers, closes her eyes, puts her lips to mine gently, like a butterfly alighting on a flower petal. My heart stutters.

She pulls me back to the moving world and we are part of the anticipatory throngs migrating loudly to the track edge. The trotters and pacers are warming up, their coats groomed to brilliance, their heads erect. They kick up clumps of dirt in their wake, clumps that seem suspended briefly, punctuating their passage. When the horses are heated to readiness, the races begin, called by a deep smooth voice that booms out over loudspeakers throughout the grounds. The voice tells us who leads on the backstretch, who passes on the far turn, who brings up the rear. The boys bet with their friends. This race I put a dollar on the sleek black, I know the farmer who drives him, he goes to our church. He leads most of the race, then falls behind, finishes fourth. I pay my bet, I must look crestfallen, because the girl I now love as I have loved no one before seems to find my defeat endearing, she says, "Aw, it's okay" and it is better than okay, she slides her arm around my waist, I can feel every molecule in the skin of her arm as it rests on my back. I think I must die now, it will never get any more lovely than this.

The races end at six and the grounds partially empty. Farm families with dairy cattle must go home to milk, but they'll be back. No such duty calls us; we are staying. The lights come on in the Palace as we enter its faded majesty to watch the pie auction. When the last Dutch Apple has been won like a trophy and carried aloft out the door, we exit too, our appetites whetted by watching pastries. The Throat, a bottomless pit of desire, leads the way, as always. An ice-cream waffle is followed by a second, by a half grilled chicken, potato salad, four cobs of corn, a large pop, more cotton candy.

The sun has been fighting to hang on above the trees at the top of the Lake Hill, but finally, wearily, sags behind them; the evening purples, then goes deep black. The Palace, lit only this one night a year now, looks like a high ship; the midway lights sparkle. We stroll, hips touching. The moon, as if on the other end of a teeter-totter with the sun, pops above the trees over the town. The perfect harvest moon for the perfect night, orange, full to bursting, come to look upon this abundance.

Fresh from work, supper, bath, people pour into the grounds. Eventually the moon rides overhead and we ride with it – the Ferris Wheel, the Tilt-a-Whirl, the Snake. She and I ride them all, repeatedly, greedy with this burgeoning love. Lights and laughter, wild movement, adrenaline. Stop, undo the safety catch, step out dizzy, try another. Finally we settle, content to meld into the crowd, to watch. She leans back into me and I encircle her with my arms. I can feel her breath, slow, satisfied, almost drowsy. I lean down to whisper in her ear. "Tomorrow do you want to...?" "Hush," she stops me. "Don't spoil now with tomorrow." She's right, I still my tongue and its plans for the rest of our lives, wrap my arms more tightly around her.

The Throat is on the Swing, two rows of seats suspended from long chains. Its riders are flung outward against the edge of possibility, more violently with each revolution, until finally they are on a plane that is nearly horizontal. Centrifugal Force – Chicky taught us that in Physics last week. The Throat's face looks strange, contracted, pained, pale even in the glow of all those coloured lights. As he whips by me we lock eyes and I see panic, I suddenly see the ugly future and try to pull the girl backwards but she resists, she is too blissful to budge, and besides, the crowd hems us in. Then all that junk the Throat has absorbed, all that long day's surfeit, rebels against constraint and forces itself up and out, aided by Centrifugal Force. As they become aware, people in the crowd begin to scream, they try to scatter, but they stumble upon themselves. With every hurled revolution of the Swing, the Throat's shame sprays outward and patters down upon the disgusted.

By the time the shocked operator has brought the Swing to a stop, and the Throat has wobbled from his seat, the immediate area is almost clear. The girl and I still stand there. When she'd finally awakened to the carnage, she'd turned around into my chest, tucked her head in and whimpered, while I did my best to shield her. Now I am brushing at her hair and clothes, trying vainly to rid her of the filth – bits of wiener, kernels of corn. She slaps my hand away, revulsed, "Don't! Don't!" and begins to weep. Just then the Throat stumbles towards us and out of his slime-encrusted lips spills, "Sorry, so sorry." He plunks down beside us, puts his head in his hands, moans. And I stand there covered in someone else's puke, paralyzed by inability to cope and by impending loss, while the girl's friends come to take her home, dabbing at her with Kleenex. "Sorry," I call after her, "so sorry," as they disappear out the big stone gates, as the lights of the Palace wink out and the big old building once again becomes its dowdy self.

FRIDAY NIGHTS

On Friday nights, the country comes to the town. Carloads of farm families spill onto the main street. The stores stay open until nine. The benches are full, and their occupants fluid. One minute the Lamonts are camped there in front of the bakery eating cookies, big golden ones with raisins, the next they have moved to the spot near the drugstore and their place has been taken by the Mackinnons. The farm men look scrubbed; they look healthy, outdoorsy, their faces wind- and sun- scoured, their beefy arms hanging loose from short-sleeved dress shirts. They look as if they would rather be back in the barn shoving cattle aside to get them milked, or wrestling a tractor around a field, or cranking barbed wire onto a pole with a come-along. They eat ice cream avidly, speak seldom, smile often.

The townies go downtown too. Or uptown. I differentiate, because it is important. It is uptown if you live below the main street and above the lake, downtown if you live on the section between the main street and the creek. The town flows downhill from the Mill Creek to the lake. Water is always the boundary. We get cleaned up and walk downtown when I live in the apartment behind the garage, uptown later when I live in a house a block below the dairy. My parents talk to everyone, they have lived here all their lives. That's the way of the place. My aunts and uncles and cousins will be there. My friends will be there. If it is between late May and September, tourists will also be arriving there for the weekend, from London and Kitchener, Toronto and Guelph, Detroit and Ypsilanti. The people that my dad built a cottage for at Goble's Grove will be there and they will greet us warmly and hand my dad a cheque. Every house in town will be left unlocked.

There is much movement, and you can stand with your back to it and see it inverted in the big plate glass windows of the stores. Car trunks will gradually fill with groceries and clothes, paint and laundry soap, cotter pins and drive belts. Someone will have for sale fat brown eggs that the next day will sizzle, their edges turning lacy and brown, alongside fresh slab bacon in a dozen iron frying pans around town, someone else a sack of hens to be later decapitated by fathers with hatchets while kids stand slack-jawed rooted to the ground by spraying blood and headless bodies caroming off walls and trees. Someone will shake his head about the lack of rain and how small the corn is and moan, "If she don't open up soon I'll hafta buy feed fer next winter." Someone else will darkly describe the hunting dog that ran one of his heifers to death the week before, and the man who owns the hound will slink away from the edge of that group, go home where he will heap curses upon the defenceless animal and beat it with a belt so that it cowers for months, then he'll go back up to the beverage room and drink tepid draft beer until his eyes no longer focus and his head lolls and his friends have to carry him home. Ice cream will drip onto freshly washed and ironed dresses, and mothers will fuss and dab at it with spit-soaked Kleenex. Two boys will throw a sponge ball back and forth over the roofs of parked and moving cars until a merchant in an apron, maybe a butcher, maybe a greengrocer, comes out to yell at them and ask if they haven't any parents and explains how his foot will feel on their behinds if they break his window. Someone elderly will have a weak spell and the doctor, who lives just steps away, will be fetched, and a crowd will gather and people will cluck about how the afflicted used to be such a strong man he could split cordwood for twelve hours straight or how she raised eleven children on her own by taking in laundry after her no-good husband up and left her for that city woman with the cottage south of town and how isn't it a shame that it has come to this state. Some may even glance up the street towards the cemetery, up near the creek, and imagine this person's name on a stone in the setting sun, and fresh-turned earth. And that gust of olfactory thought will lead to the harrowing that needs doing tomorrow. Then the doctor, who is in his eighties, and whose hand shakes like fear itself before he gives you your shots, and whose hair, while still all there, is white, and who delivered you and your mother too, works his way through the concerned crowd to attend to the old man or old woman, who is judged to be fine. Is there someone who can drive him/her home? And a dozen offers are made, and then the crowd disperses, and the two sides of the four commerical blocks of the main street are again ebb and flow, until about nine, first one merchant then the next comes out to lower an awning and bring in a door mat and turn out the lights. If the night is fair, and it always seems to be, small knots of the reluctant will stay gathered after the last store is shut up, then they too give it up. Gradually the street slows its breathing and reclaims itself.

Chris' first Christmas, 1963. Chris (6 months) in front.
Rear, left to right: John (6) with knight's lance, Roger (14), Jim (12).

BLACK AND WHITE

The world before TV is one of long, rain-pattered afternoons in the porch with comics, of shapeless play until the evening baths and parents force us into sleep. It is radio serials after supper, dreamy me lying on my parents' bed listening to the Masked Man and Tonto save the world from desperados. The word *desperado* makes my blood run cold. I imagine mesas and buttes and skies that go on forever.

Then one couple has this new device. The whole town is buzzing with the news. Charlie and Lil Schell's TV is hooked to a tall antenna higher than their big English Cherry tree and Norwegian Spruce. It pulls in, sometimes feeble and snowy, but watchable nonetheless, Buffalo, whose test pattern is an Indian head. Once or twice a week Charlie and Lil welcome a group of us into their home where waiting for us are Howdy Doody and the Mickey Mouse Club. Lil gives us milk in big glasses and fresh cookies still warm from her oven. It will spoil our suppers that await us, so she warns us not to tell our moms. We will do anything for Lil; our lips are sealed. Clarabell the Clown can't speak, but he can communicate via the horns he wears around his waist. He squirts people with a seltzer bottle. Buffalo Bob, with his western shirt and bolo tie, is the hero, in love with the beautiful Indian Princess, Summerfall, who wears buckskin. Phineus T.Bluster is like the crusty old man who yells at us on the way to school. There is silly Dilly Dally. And Howdy, in his checked shirt, is freckled and grins like the village idiot. We sit slack-jawed in front of this faraway world.

Then the Flemings up our street get television. After school my little brother Jim and I begin going there for Krazy Kat and Mighty Mouse. Their big dog joins the four of us on the floor in the living room. Sometimes we feed him dog biscuits; sometimes we too eat the hard treats, first softening them with our saliva. The Fleming boys' mom, Jean, can never figure why they are always short of these treats. Krazy loves Ignatz Mouse. Ignatz repays Krazy's adoration by throwing bricks at Krazy's head. It is our early introduction to the cut and thrust of relationships. That other rodent, Mighty Mouse, loves Pearl Pureheart, but his heart is stolen by the exotic Krakatoa Katy. This is during what may be Mighty's most wonderful accomplishment: throwing a lasso around the neck of the volcano and snugging it shut before it can destroy everything. Krakatoa expands, burps loudly, swells again, then subsides. Katy leans up and gives MM a hug and smooch. Mighty's chest swells. The Flemings' dog farts contentedly.

And then one day the world changes again. When I arrive home from school, parked in the driveway is the truck from Lakeshore Electronics. The two Reany brothers are muscling a large box up the stairs and in through the side door. I rush inside to watch wordlessly and impatiently from a corner while they un-crate the TV and run a wire out the window. One climbs to the roof's peak to install the antenna, then they fiddle with the reception. The one below yells out the window, "More to the west. Nope, back a bit, a bit more, almost, almost." Almost, almost, please be finished soon, I am almost *dying*. Then they nod at me, at my mother, it is done, they shut it off, leave. We turn it back on, my mother and I, just as my dad walks in the door from work. We three stand there as the screen goes from dark, to blur, to snow. Then, in front of our eyes, the future comes slowly into focus.

A SAFE EDGE

I am chewing thoughtfully on the end of my pencil. I look down at the indentations my teeth have made in the yellow painted wood. I wonder if my grandfather the dentist would be displeased with me, given the disreputable state of my mouth. The pencil wood is soft and releases a faint cedar scent each time I crunch down on it. I wonder how they get the graphite core inside the pencil, then how they get the caramel inside the pockets of Caramilk chocolate bars.

I am deep in the middle of my Grade Ten Shop exam. Though I am not skilled in shop, except perhaps in drafting, I like the hands-on stuff, the sawing, sanding, staining, shellacking, the holding of a gouge to a spinning piece of wood and watching form emerge from bluntness, the applying of a dull chisel to a whirling wheel at just such an angle that it is whetted sharp enough to shave hair off your arm. But the theoretical part of Shop is boring to me. I have answered questions so far about rabbeting, dovetailing, coving and chamfering, identified the parts of the table saw and their functions, told about the process for building a fire in a forge. Now I am being asked to draw a diagram explaining how I would measure, scratch, snip, then fold a piece of tin into a box of certain dimensions. I begin my drawing, stop, chew, remember that I must make allowances for folding. I gnaw, I draw, erase, and what I end up with isn't bad, a box one could be proud of. I'm done with the exam, just look things over one last time. As I do, I curse, look around to make sure I have contained the expletive within my head, but Dusty Rhodes, our teacher, isn't diverted from his staring out the window at the traffic passing on Goderich Street. Crap! A safe edge, I have forgotten to allow for a safe edge. Our book tells us you must make a quarter-inch fold around the top of the box, thus increasing the length and width of the material needed by a half-inch. Without this safety measure any box you make becomes a gaping wound waiting to happen. I mutter angrily, but this time I must do it aloud because Dusty is giving me a hard stare and my friend in the adjacent row is looking inquisitively at me. I heave a mighty sigh, take a fresh sheet of paper, start drawing anew. This one doesn't, for some reason, turn out as well, but I'm out of time so it'll have to do. Shortly Dusty clears his throat, announces, "Time's up, gentlemen," and it's out the door.

To where we meet a grim-faced principal and vice-principal. "I regret to inform you..." The principal stops, clears his throat, begins again. "I regret to inform you that at 1:30 p.m., in Dallas, the American president, John F. Kennedy, was shot." There is stunned silence. "We let you finish your exam before passing along this sad news. The buses have been called and will depart early. Those of you from town, go home now."

The halls are usually bedlam after exams let out, but what voices there are around me are muffled and slurred like a 78 rpm record played at 45. I labour to get home. It isn't far, only a block and a half, but gravity has mysteriously increased and my legs are almost glued to the earth.

At the front door I can hear my mother sobbing. She is standing in front of the television weeping and ironing, on the table beside her, a cigarette burning in an ashtray and a half-drunk bottle of Coca Cola. I stand watching her as she irons with mechanical precision. Even in our underwear there are no wrinkles. She does this job, as she does all her housework, with rigorous pride. When she realizes I am there, she sets the iron down on end, rushes to me and enfolds me in a teary hug. "He's dead." When I left the school the final word wasn't yet out, but I feared the worst. "It could be the beginning of the Third World War," wails my mom. "They say tanks are massing in East Germany on its border with the West. They say the Communists are behind this." I try to hush her, but it will not work, I know, she has already seen a war, firmly believes she will see another.

We sit and watch the sombre faces on the black and white screen. The broadcasts are funereal; a Canadian commentator urges us to remain calm, but it does nothing to soothe us. I feel like I have been gutted. My middle two brothers come home. The older of the two, Jim, has some sense of all this, and he sits down, staring with us at Dealey Plaza, the Texas School Book Depository, a progression of crumpled faces being interviewed; the younger, John, goes out to play. My baby brother, Chris, just five months old, slumbers on in his crib. As it gets dark my mom's instincts kick in; she stumbles to the kitchen; she is a wonderful cook but tonight she slides TV dinners into the oven for supper. She brings down the baby and feeds him. My little brother comes in all leafy and dirty from play. She doesn't say anything to him. We peel back the foil from our meals, we eat automatically, without tasting. We do not leave the television.

They have arrested someone. He killed a policeman but they got him. Oswald. "I wish your father was here," Mom blurts out, and I realize what day it is, November 22, their wedding anniversary. Every year since he and his friends bought their hunt camp on Manitoulin Island, my dad has missed their anniversary. She normally laughs when it comes up, says she doesn't care. But today she does. Just then the phone rings, it is my father, calling to wish her happy anniversary. He hasn't heard; they just got in from cleaning and hanging the deer. I imagine the hunt camp: men unshaven and tired, their hands still sticky with blood. Sitting having a drink with their guns leaning quiet now against the wall. Their dogs fed and curled with satisfaction by the fire. The deer outside, suspended by their heels from a high bar out of the reach of bears and wolves, their body cavities emptied, their eyes staring sightlessly at the faraway ground. I imagine my father driving back from town and the pay phone, bringing them the news.

Whatever my dad has said to my mom calms her. She has ceased weeping. The middle two brothers are now doing their homework at the table. My baby brother, Chris, is in my lap looking up at me. My mother and I are still in front of the TV and she has resumed her ironing. She does it long into the night. She tugs and straightens, flattens and smoothes, works the nose of the iron into the tiniest corners, as if rooting out evil. Every shirt, every pair of pants, every dish towel, steamed, pressed. Order being restored.

THE BAD BOYS

The bad boys live up the street, between our house and our friends'. To go up there to play or to watch Mighty Mouse, we must pass through their purview. Dangerous territory, where they seem to always wait. I know the Lord's Prayer, have been forced to learn it in Sunday School, have heard it repeated solemnly many times. Each time I approach the bad boys' place, I hear in my head, "Yea, though I walk through the valley of the shadow of death, I shall fear no evil." Only I do fear bad boy evil.

They throw words, curses surprisingly sharp for ones so young. My mother says that it is no wonder, given their home life, but I don't know what she means. I am overly sensitive and their profanity and taunts sting me, sometimes make me cry. They wait with more than that, baskets of hard green apples, or worse, piles of stones or chunks of pavement prised up from the edge of the street.

Every trip up the street for us, or down for our friends, is a trial. As we approach their corner, the bad boys, four brothers and their kitty corner friend, lean back, yell, "Fire" and heave. Then bend down to re-arm, heave again. A rain of stone or unripe fruit descends around and upon us. We run, looking up always, judging trajectory, dodging. I have seen a film called *Giants of the Marathon*, where the famed warriors launched a hail of javelins that blackened the sky and descended upon the pitiable enemy with a vengeance. This is our daily epic. They live between us and our goal, thus becoming our enemies, simple as that. There are other streets we could take, go around them, but we are drawn to that passage. It has become their job to impede our free movement and our duty to blast through their barricade, get where we are going. We learn to fight back, pulling behind us a wagon filled with gravel that we wing by the handful, bigger stones that lack the scattershot effectiveness of gravel but do much worse than sting if they land. Two bunches of grubby little boys stand feet apart and hurl hatred until someone runs out of ammunition or someone's courage falters in the face of a particularly withering broadside. The victors howl, the losers retreat.

Occasionally they leave their patch of turf to strike out. One summer day my brother and I, supervised by our babysitter, are in a tent constructed of old quilts and lawn chairs in our back yard. We are having a party; she has made us lemonade and cupcakes, chocolate ones with white icing, white ones with chocolate frosting, a half maraschino cherry topping each. We are singing, laughing, shoving sweetness into our mouths. Then all is descending darkness and chaos as the blankets crash down upon us and we hear derisive laughter. Our babysitter ploughs out into the sunlight. Though she is older, they are brazen; they do not run from her, just stand snickering at the cupcake crushed onto her chest. "You cruel, brainless bastards," she yells. They reply with shameful things, dirty things, sexual things which we don't really understand but which we know are not to be spoken aloud in the company of girls. She stands, fists balled up, her face red and tear-streaked, as they saunter, satisfied and hooting, back up the street.

Another time, after we have arrived at his house badly shaken by an encounter with the bad boys, our friends' father marches down the street to their place and berates them. He calls them hooligans, scoundrels, thugs, criminals. He says they need thrashing. In silence they let him have his say, but their eyes are shining. The next day when he backs his car out of the driveway to go to church, he hears the crunch of breaking glass, gets out to see broken beer bottles under all four tires, two of which are slowly subsiding onto their rims.

It all ends the day one of them, a young one, works his way down the street and sidles up to us where we are playing on the front lawn. He isn't supposed to be there. A few weeks ago he hit my brother in the forehead with the tines of a garden rake my dad had left out. My mom sent him packing. We look up warily, but he is smiling guilelessly, we let our guard down. He is sneaky quick, grabbing my brother's wrist, biting him hard on the underside of the forearm, on the meat, drawing blood. Then he hightails it towards home. My brother's screams bring my mother out the kitchen door; we babble what happened and she sprints off up the street, tea towel still in hand. We follow, curious. He is fast but she is faster, spurred on by maternal anger, and she pulls him up short by the collar of his shirt. He kicks and squirms, trying to slip her grasp, but to no avail. "Want to know what it feels like?" she spits. His eyes grow large. She roughly seizes his arm, chomps down on it. He howls. She lets him go, and home he scampers. A moment later, as my mother has turned to my brother and is tending his wound with the towel, the bad boys' mother bangs out her screen door and ends up toe to toe with my mom. They are both shrieking, blaming. Then my mom yells that the next time one of the bad boys so much as looks sideways at us, she'll call the police and have the whole detestable brood thrown into *Reform School*, where they *belong*. Which makes their mom shut her mouth hard, turn away, go back inside.

We move not too long after to the other side of town and the bad boys cease to be a regular part of our lives. I no longer wake up sweating, feeling their stones descend upon me like hail. I see them in the schoolyard, but there they are just other kids in a yard full of kids. They hold marbles in their hands, or softballs. They no longer hold my wildly beating heart.

BURN 2

The main street is perhaps eighty feet wide, the sidewalk fifteen, and as the hardware store burns, it seems that every curious inhabitant of the town is crowded into the confines of those fifteen feet opposite the action.

Men play water into the ground-floor store, occasionally switching to the blasted-in windows of the second storey apartment and the abutting walls of the structures on either side. This building may be a loss but they must stop it from involving the entire downtown. Fire is rabid, excited, it wants to jump, wants to implicate the whole world in its horseplay.

It is always night when the best fires happen, as if the arranger of conflagrations is a painter who knows the value of contrast. There is nothing better than orange, yellow and red sinuous against that onyx sky, flames brighter and much more immediate than those cold blue distant suns with no life revolving around them.

My father is inside somewhere, my mother watches, fretting. Her fingers flex, relax, flex, her nails work our shoulders where we stand in front of her. She keeps repeating, "Jesus, Jesus, Jesus," and I don't know if she is praying or swearing softly to herself. He disappeared into that second-floor apartment window, scrambling up a ladder after someone shouted something about an infant in there, something about a baby carriage. No one wants to think about that, a baby, only months old, alone, crying, heat and fire and smoke inching their inexorable way, like big slow snakes towards their prey.

I can feel her breath whoosh out when my father appears at the window, a carriage in his arms. He drops it to men waiting below, fathers who are gentle men and who catch it as if it is the most precious jewel in the world, lower it to the ground, wheel it away. The crowd lets whoop a collective cheer and my father's form slides back into the window's darkness and my mother's hands tighten onto our shoulders again, and then a moment later relax, there he is again, safe on the flat roof, and his fellows smoothly run a long ladder to him and he descends it in no apparent haste, although the second floor is now alight, and then he touches the ground. Another fire-fighter stops him, says something to him, he nods, and sprints across the street to us, a big loose grin on his face, a sheepish grin.

He shakes his head ruefully. There never was a baby in there, the mother had it all along, what he saved was the doll and doll carriage of the youngest daughter, but in that smoke, in that haste, who could tell? He is laughing and my mother is crying, but their little drama becomes secondary because, across the street the pent-up bombs of all those paint cans in that store have begun to finally jig to life and are launching up into the night like some pyrotechnician's handiwork, arcing wildly and exploding above a play that has hours yet to run before it dissolves into a puddle of daylight and sooty water.

COOL 2

We have all seen the Beatles, the way they shake their heads when they trill *ooooooooooo* on *She Loves You* and the way the long fringe of hair on their foreheads sways. It is cool and our parents don't like it and we crave it, want to feel that swish of hair across our own foreheads as we make girls scream the way they do on the Ed Sullivan Show. But brush-cuts and duck's asses and Brylcreem are still in. My dad is bald, has been almost forever, so I take his prohibition in our family of long hair as jealousy on his part. But I toe the line.

Louis is the first in our high school to grow his hair. He has a lump on his forehead, some kind of rogue cyst, and wants to cover it, and he wants to be a Beatle too, of course, everyone does. You don't notice hair growing, right? It's like fingernails, one day they are fine and one day they seem just past the limit. Just one day he comes to class and his bangs are down to his eyebrows. Some girl goes right up to him and runs her fingers through it and a big smile cracks his face open. We all admire, all wish we had his guts, his hair.

The principal and vice-principal do not admire. They are hard cases. Girls don't wear pants, guys can't wear jeans. And long hair will sap the pith from our brains, apparently. They haul Louis out of period one English right in the middle of *Porphyria's Lover*, you know, the poem where the whacko strangles his girlfriend with her long tresses so she will be his forever. They take him to the office and sit him down and both lean over him, just like in cop movies, no doubt they shine a light in his eyes, and they tell him that he won't come to school the next day unless he's trimmed his hair. *Understood?* He tells them he understands.

These guys are not to be toyed with, I know. Once, in Grade Nine math, I laughed, and the VP, who was our math teacher, nailed me with his eyes so I sobered right up. He hauled me into his office at noon. He stood over me, his silver tooth glinting. He too was bald and had a big scar running from near his eye to up over his forehead. I thought it might be from a sabre cut suffered in the Crimean War. "Do you think math is funny?" he inquired. I have a big mouth, am known to shoot from the lip, and before I could rein it in, I replied, "Nope, *definitely* nothing funny *at all* about math." He might be old and bald and teach math but he knew sarcasm when it slapped him and I knew I was in deep when he shoved his face into mine and hissed, "Care to repeat that impertinent remark?" He had a reputation for having strapped five Grade Thirteen boys for impertinence. I swallowed hard, gulped out, "Sorry," and scrambled gratefully from that tightness, having lived to tell the tale.

We all want to know from Louis what happened, what he will do now. He just smiles endearingly, makes the girls' hearts melt, makes the guys want to cluster around him and protect him from the forces of adult evil. "Don't worry," he says.

I get to school unusually early the next day. I want to be there when his bus comes in. He steps cheerily off the bus; nothing has changed, the fringe is still the same length as yesterday. Oh god, they'll kill him, they'll strap him. I tell him that. He smiles softly. "Don't think so," he says, and pulls out an envelope from his binder. "Secret weapon," is all he says, and heads for the office, whistling. He is so cool, he is like the Light Brigade.

I love the idea of martyrdom, so I follow, to bear his broken body back. He enters the Valley of Death and five minutes later out he comes, not martyred at all, grinning broadly. His secret weapon was in the envelope, a letter from his doctor saying that "Louis is highly embarrassed by his forehead lump and needs the long hair to maintain his self-esteem." A get out of jail free card is what it is! Free Parking! He gets to keep his hair.

And the precedent is set; two weeks later another guy comes in with a letter from his mom excusing his shaggy look because he has a huge hockey scar on his head where an errant puck opened him up. Soon there is hair anarchy. I don't immediately follow suit; the reason I give myself is that my hair is too curly, but I know it's really my father and the disapproving wrinkling of that chrome dome of his that keeps me from being a Mop Top, that prevents all those wonderful, wild girls from shrieking my name and fainting every time I shimmy and go *ooooooooooooooo*.

Saugeen District High School 1965-66 Soccer Team,
Roger front left, pointy shoes, tight black pants, white socks,
skinny leather tie, all very cool.

YOU SHOULD BE GLAD

When first I hear that Beatles' song on the radio, I am instantly ecstatic, whirling around the bedroom. It's a *gotta have*. I thump downstairs, leap on my bike and pedal furiously up to Ernie's drug store, which is kitty-corner to the other drugstore, run by Jack. My mom buys drugs from Jack; she used to work in that store when she was younger and it was run by Luckhams; she is therefore fiercely loyal to it. When I was small I would go in just to watch Jack grind things with his mortar and pestle. My fascination now lies at Ernie's, where I buy my records. If he doesn't have what you want, he orders it in for you.

Directly inside the front door are bins filled with the latest 45s, each nestling inside its paper cover so that you can pick it up and check out the labels. There is the red of RCA Victor with the dog stuffing his head into the gramophone, the more austere blue and silver of Philips and of London, the black and silver of Chess, the gold of Parkway and REO, the burgundy of Apex, the sunbright yellow with the word EPIC inside a black oval sunburst, and the circus rainbow of Decca. But what I am looking for this day is the spirals of orange and yellow that signal Capitol. When you have those records on the turntable and look down at them the colours swirl seductively.

"Do you have *She Loves You*?" I breathlessly ask Ernie. "Do we?" he demands of his daughter, who is working in the back. When she comes up front, searches through the bins, my knees grow weak. She's ahead of me in school, very smart, very cute. Green-eyed and freckled. I feel faint around girls like that. In fact, I grow faint around *all* girls right now. I am looking at the pale white backs of her knees below the hem of her plaid skirt. She turns, smiles at me and for a minute I forget why I'm there until I see the paper sleeve she's holding out to me. "Our only copy," she says. "You're the first in town to have it." And she smiles again at me so hard every hormonal pimple on my red face feels as if it might burst. Before that happens and adds to my humiliation, I mumble my thanks, take the record to Ernie, pay my dollar and race home again, up the stairs, snap the little yellow hole spacer into the record, slide it over the spindle, let it drop, swing the tone arm over, hold my breath as it descends into place, and the Mop-Tops explode from the speaker.

All afternoon, over and over and over, I play *She Loves You*. My father yells up the stairs that maybe I want to give it a break, play something else. I play the B side, *I'll Get You*. I play it twice, lose interest, go back to A. Yeah yeah yeah. Infectious. Around and around spiral the orange and yellow. I love this music, almost all music, have ever since I was confined for most of the summer with red measles and my main companion was CKLW, playing mostly country music during the day then rock at night. And, when the sun went down, distant rock stations like WXYZ in New York and WGR, the Goodwill Station in Chicago, became clear. The music is in me like some happy disease. I'm glad all over, just like the Dave Clark Five sing.

I'm in bits and pieces of ecstasy. I listen avidly in those precious moments before I have to get out of bed in the morning, after school out in the yard on our new Japanese transistor radio, at night while I wade through Latin and math. I tackle the chapter called "The Dress of a Roman Woman" (which the book's previous owner has cleverly altered to "The *Un*Dress*ing* of a Roman Woman") while Bobby Vee croons that "she wore blue velvet"; I imagine Ernie's daughter wearing blue velvet, then wearing nothing...and though there is no one there to see it, my face goes scarlet. I rip through parabolic equations with Jan and Dean, not backing off on Dead Man's Curve. I read the word *subsumed* in a book recently. Music has subsumed me, and what a drowning it is.

My mother knocks on my door interrupting my umpteenth playing of the record. "Fred is downstairs for you." I go down to where Fred waits. He is tall and twitchy and has big hair. He wants to be a disc jockey in Toronto, and he is even more mad for music than I am. "Is it true?" he asks. "Is what true?" I know exactly what he means but I want to drag out his pain. I also read the word *schadenfreude* recently. "Is it true that you are the only one in town with *She Loves You*?" "Yep." "I gotta have it," he begs; I think he'd fall on his knees before me and wrap his long arms around my calves and kiss my feet if my parents weren't here. "I'll give you five bucks for it." Is he nuts? I hesitate. "I just bought it, Fred." "Okay, then..." he licks his lips, "Ten bucks," and he whips a tenner out of his pocket, proffers it. God, he really *does* need it.

My mom interrupts, "But Fred, you can just-" I cut her off by snatching his money and saying, "Follow me." I know what she is going to say, he can just go up to the drugstore and order it and have it in two days. But he needs it now and I need to profit from his mania. We get to my room, and when he looks at the turntable his face nearly splits with the grin. "One last time," I say, "then it's all yours." He nods, too overcome to speak. I play it, slide it off the spindle and into its sleeve, hand it to him. No kidding, he is trembling so much he can barely hold onto it. I am too as I fondle the ten in my pocket. "Now you are the only one in town with *She Loves You*," I say as I herd him down the stairs and out the front door. As soon as he's turned the corner, I am on my way back up to the drugstore. Ernie's daughter is behind the counter. She smiles, but I do not falter this time, I am on a mission. "I'd like to order a copy of *She Loves You*," I say. She looks quizzically at me, I slap down the ten dollar bill, "and," I add emphatically, the greatest wheeler dealer of all time, "I want *Wipeout* by the Surfaris and *I Get Around* by the Beach Boys and *Surf City* by Jan and Dean and *It's Judy's Turn to Cry* by Leslie Gore and *It's Over* by Roy Orbison..." "Will you slow down?" she says, "I can't write that fast." I add, more slowly, four more discs. "They'll be here in two days," she says.

And they are. My collection of 45s has just doubled. Yeah yeah yeah mixes with the percussive insistence of *Wipeout* and Roy Orbison's strings-backed breakup tears and the sweet harmonies of the Beach Boys. For two days Fred has been happy, the only one in town... "It was worth the ten bucks," he says to me after I tell him he is no longer the sole owner, and he isn't just trying to justify his impulsiveness. It *was* worth it. Some things just are.

IT'S OVER

I am not my brother. He is heart-throb handsome and has girls all over him. A friend of my dad says enviously that my brother has so many young women interested in him he has to "beat them off with a stick." I have no such problems. I have lots of guy friends. I even have girl friends. But no *girlfriend.* It's the space between the words that counts most. I watch my brother closely for his secret, but I can never discern anything other than his blonde Beatle cut and baby blue eyes and easy smile. My hair is wavy and reddish-brown, I am nowhere near as good-looking, I have lots of pimples. But my smile is nice, I've been told, and I too have blue eyes and I do way better in school than he does. So what? None of that seems to matter, not with girls.

I think I long for love excessively. My mother says to be patient, it will happen. I don't believe her. I'm her son, of course she says that because she loves me, she pities me. I've read all the Greek myths and I know that the Greek gods punished those who desired. Golden Fleece, no? I think I am being punished for desiring soft lips on mine and breasts pressed up against me. I think the reason I get stupid and clumsy and red-faced every time a girl and I are close is that I am a loser who is destined to live womanless into old age and I'll end up sprawled on a sunny bench somewhere uptown the way the local geezers do, horking and spitting and taking out their false teeth to compare and gabbing about the lack of rain and how they can't eat corn on the cob or steak anymore and have you heard the garbage kids these days call music?

But, though I am loathe to admit it, my mother is right. Finally, in Grade Twelve, it happens. She is new to the school, I ask someone her name, that someone tells her. Next thing, she walks right up to me. Bold. Foxy. She wears clingy mini-skirts and trendy striped hose. She has hazel eyes, curly hair, and she sees something in me that I can't, because the next thing I know we are walking hand in hand down the halls every morning after her bus arrives. I used to leave for school five minutes before classes started, eating toast as I hurried up the street. Now I am there an hour early, waiting, anticipating how her hand will feel when it settles in mine, how our elbows will nudge, our shoulders touch. Nothing we talk about as we walk registers, my body simply knows that I am attached to someone solid and something vital is flowing between us. Lockers blur, dust motes dance in the shafts of morning sun coming in the tall windows. People are talking all around us; it should be noisy but I'm so into her aura that all I hear is a dull murmur, like wind in the poplars. Other students smile at us as we go by, teachers nod; we have become an item.

We can't get enough of each other. A school day isn't sufficient. I took *Romeo and Juliet* in English last year and I understood full well what the Friar meant when he warned Romeo that "the sweetest honey is loathsome in his own deliciousness." I am addled and consequences mean nothing. I phone her each night, but she sounds far. I need touch. She lives five miles north, in the next town up the highway. Sometimes I drive my parents' car to visit, sometimes I hitchhike; once while thumbing, I don't get rides either way but the five-mile walk each direction seems barely to exist. The way up is all anticipation, the way back all sweet dwelling upon what she said, did. Not that we do much. Kissing. A lot of holding and listening to each other breathe. Still, her father is suspicious of me. Her sister, my age but much more worldly than I, is friendly. Her mother is warm and always makes me something to eat before I head home, saying, "You can't go all that way on an empty stomach." But her father is aloof, seems to want to trap me in some lie I have no intention of telling. He seldom leaves us alone, like a gamekeeper who knows a potential poacher when he sees one. We have to go for walks along the river to escape his presence; we go down to where the Saugeen empties into the lake, then south along the shore to the beach and sit on a log looking out at the water. We talk about something, we talk about nothing. My hip bumps against hers, my left arm is around her shoulders, her right around my ribs. The waves, as they have always done, slide in, disappear, head out. How far? Don't know, don't care. Somewhere out there they re-reverse and come back. Our shoes are off, our toes dig holes in the sand, sand that was once rock, a million years ago. The sun drops tantalizingly, the west turns red with desire, then pink, then violet, and the light of the Chantry Island lighthouse blinks on and begins to warn of danger. She sighs, stands, pulls me up, clasps me hard to her, kisses me, says, "Time to go back." And through the purple dusk we amble back to her house, where the lights have come on like beacons and her sister sits at the kitchen table doing homework and her mother is reading *Wuthering Heights* and her father is sitting in his wing-chair supposedly listening to the radio but probably imagining me as Heathcliff.

All the fractiousness of the teenage years that has driven my parents crazy has disappeared. My grandfather winks at me and jokes about puppy love, my grandmother bakes me my favourite oatmeal cookies as if I have accomplished something major, my friends, though I now ignore them often and turn down offers to indulge in idleness with them, approve, support me silently. All I desire is this, a little taste of this joy; well, I'd like a bit more, yes, what teenage boy doesn't want that shirt to unbutton, that pale breast to fit into his hand like a tender bird, those legs to open freely on the gift of that Golden Fleece? And who doesn't think that maybe this leads to forever, that years from now there will be a home filled with the laughter of children, a house with green lawns and croquet and warm kitchen smells.

So it comes hard and swift and very painfully when she tells me one fine spring day out on the back steps of the school that it's over, that "something isn't working anymore." She is crying, but I'm not, not yet. I am just so stunned. I think she tells me more, maybe gives me reasons, but I have gone deaf, all I can hear is from deep inside, the ripping open of my heart, all I can feel is that death-heavy wash of blood filling me to drowning. I stumble to my feet and zombie-walk back inside the school. And there is her sister, who says nothing, but touches me gently on the arm and her eyes tell me she knows. She told her sister before she told me? Chemistry class is a fog, not one equation will solve, history is all about long-lost wars. The school spills its guts out at 3:30 and I go home, directly to my room, close the door behind me, sit heavily on the bed. I know I should cry, so I do. I have inherited my mom's histrionic side, and today I do that justice. I cry until I think there is no more water in my body. Then I get up and put on Roy Orbison's *It's Over* and play it again and again and again, lifting the arm before the next song on the album begins and setting it back at the beginning. I force myself to listen to all that heartache repeat itself. The speakers spew their agony:

> All the rainbows in the sky
> start to weep and say goodbye.
> you won't be seeing rainbows
> anymore.

There is a pregnant pause between lines three and four to increase the hurt.

My mother knocks at the door. "Supper is ready. Come on down, son." I imagine she knows. Yes, she will, for sure, in this goddam little shit-hole every goddam nosey body knows every goddam thing immediately. Well, I don't want her pity; all I want is Roy Orbison and self-pity. I stay in my mourning room. I don't go to the phone when my best friend calls. I don't turn on the lights as dusk arrives. I don't touch my homework. I just stand at the window overlooking the vacant lot and play that bloody song over and over, stabbing myself with it in the chest like Juliet, except I drive the knife in deep, pull it out, do it again. It hurts both directions, and double the pain is better.

> Setting suns before they fall
> recount to you, 'That's all, that's all.'

The weeping violins behind Roy swell to the climax, and the waves on the lake continue their cycle, and the snare drum goes rata-tat-tat, rata-tat-TAT! The way that drumstick snaps down guillotine hard on that last syllable of song, the clean cut to nothing, I know, it *is* over, that *is* all.

Roger's mother, Bernice Rushton (reclining on the right), with friend Della Rae (left) in front of Tuck Shop.

POP

The pop machine sits outside the office of the Uptown Motel. When I flip up the heavy metal lid, often needing two hands to do so, it sucks away from the gasket, almost unwillingly, as if the miserly machine is hesitant to give up its contents. Inside, in the well filled with hand-numbingly cold water, hang rows of six ounce pop bottles.

I take two fingers and slide a bottle gently along the track towards me. When it gets almost to the end, I put my nickel into the slot and the jaws at the end of the track relax long enough for me to extract the treasure. I close the lid with a satisfying thud, as if I have really accomplished something. In the upper left hand corner of the long front side of the machine is a receptacle. I insert the bottle at a forty-five degree angle, feel a catch, and push down. Another sucking sound, then a fizz, then a clink as the disenfranchised cap tumbles to join its friends.

I raise the bottle to my ready lips, tip it up. So cold. So sweet. The sun nearly blinds with its beauty. My teeth ache, that's how good it is. That's how good it always is.

The kid who comes up from Pittsburgh every summer calls it *soda.* I think of soda crackers, loaded with butter and pushed whole into my face. Or my grandpa Rushton slicing cool coins of kielbasa with his Swiss Army knife, then laying them almost ceremoniously on soda crackers, in a row, to be eaten as desired. But everyone here calls it *pop*, a much more onomatopoeic name. *Pop* for the sound of the top popping off. *Pop* for the bubbles that burst inside the mouth and nose. *Pop* for the sound the bottle makes when hurled against a wall so it explodes like a new galaxy into a million blue-green shards, one of which somehow comes straight at me and etches a half-moon into my forehead just above the right eye.

I go with my grandfather once a week to Seiffert's garage to get pop. They keep it in wooden crates in the cellar so you have to lift a trap door, climb down wooden stairs. There is Fanta and Crush and Coke and Pepsi. This is where I want to be trapped if there is an atomic war. I could live forever on pop. The bottles clank as they are lifted up and out. If I hold them against the skin of my cheek, I can feel they are already fridge-cool. The lime is sublime. My grandpa loves grape, as does my cousin Doug from Owen Sound, who teaches me to make grape floats. Three scoops of Mackenzies' vanilla ice cream in a tall thin glass, then grape pop gurgled over top, much fizzing and foaming, some stirring, then a seductive mix to be spooned into your ever-eager maw. No nutritional value, but what ecstasy.

Six ounces is sufficient. Six ounces costs five cents, a single coin. If things are smaller then they are more manageable. Six ounces is the perfect amount to divide between me and my younger brother. Each Saturday night, in front of the hockey game, we are allowed to split a six-ounce coke and a small bag of chips. The chips too cost five cents. There is a uniformity to things, a predictability. The chips are plain, and we add vinegar to the bag, which is then shaken. The best chips are the last, the sodden ones, the stinging ones. We take turns drinking the vinegar from the bag. I am older, so I'm in charge of the coke-splitting. I am devious, giving my brother a taller, thinner glass, and keeping the squat one. "Look," I say to him, "I'm giving you more; see how much higher it is in your glass." And he smiles, he trusts me completely. He shouldn't.

For some reason beyond my ability to fathom, the price goes up to six cents, a major complication originating somewhere outside my sphere of influence. There is a certain symmetry, yes, six cents for six ounces, but it now requires change, more than one coin. One coin can be held hotly in a curled hand, safely, sweatily, but two coins slide together, two coins breed discontent. They slip against each other, they conspire to escape, maybe fall down a sewer grate. Their friction wears holes in pockets. Still, it is the way things are now. The New World Order. I adapt. I carry more money. I gain weight.

The ten-ounce bottle may be the end of the world. We need only six ounces, we want only six ounces. But someone somewhere had decided we want more, we need more. The pop in these bottles tastes different, everyone swears it does, and if everyone says it, it must be right. The upside is, I am back to one coin, the tiniest of all, the thin dime, the merest whisper of money. Worth more, weighs less. The predictability is wavering, so it doesn't seem very long before a thin dime isn't enough, it becomes twelve, then fifteen cents, there goes the cent an ounce rule. Suddenly, we aren't getting more, we're getting less per cent, and nothing will ever be the same again. The centre cannot hold.

The machine is now in front of the Lucky Dollar Store at the main corner. It is no longer water-filled and horizontal. The new upright has a long narrow door, with the tops of bottles facing the buyer one above the other, each held at the neck by a vise. Put in your money and then you may select one bottle, pull it straight out. My friends and I realize that it is much more vulnerable than the old type, though. We see the fatal flaw. We all read science fiction, so we know that all machines mankind invents, even robots, have *a fatal flaw*. The lock on every bottle releases when the money is inserted. Theoretically, each bottle of the eight is, at once, free. When one is yanked the others re-lock, but if all were tugged at the same moment, exactly evenly, wouldn't all eight slide out? It is our mandate to try.

We look like some weird appendaged sideways-cantilevered totem pole. At first, there isn't the synchronicity needed. One is all we get. Someone is always an adrenalined heartbeat ahead of the others. But after about a week of practising, a week of bending our bodies so eight hands rest on eight bottle necks, while our own necks crane to watch for passersby, or cops, or parents, a week of learning to breath as one organism, we get three. Three pops for 15 cents, half a cent per ounce. Some sort of justice, perverted by our selfishness, is restored. We have reversed time. We make it to five once, though three or four is the norm. Then, one magic October night, with a moon as big as all get out, with air almost summer warm though it is past Thanksgiving, we manage six. Six in one pull, a quarter of a cent per ounce. Some of us will never again in our lives work as closely as this with fellow humans. Some will never experience this pinnacle of achievement. We know that we have done all that is humanly possible, that only Spider man's arch-enemy, Doctor Octopus, eight arms attuned to one brain, could beat this. We stop, and the Lucky Dollar Store resumes its pop profits, although soon after, it closes down anyway. Perhaps we sped it on its way to its demise, I do not know. Or care.

THE WORLD WITHIN THE BOX

Weekdays it comes on at 3 o'clock, signs off at ten, weekends it starts in the morning and lasts longer, as if weekdays are winter and the weekend is the longer, more generous summer. In those narrow hours everything happens. CKNX, Wingham, is the only station one can get with an ordinary aerial. We watch all it has to offer.

There is Circle 8 Ranch with Cora and the Cowboys. "Toe-tappin' music," Dad says, grabbing Mom and whirling her around the room. There's Lassie, everyone's dream dog. Every week the loveable but hapless Timmy tumbles down an abandoned well or into a raging river and every week Lassie drags a rope or a reluctant Grandpa ("What is it girl, what's wrong?") to the site of the disaster and Timmy is saved. Lassie's fine but I favour Yukon King, the trusty canine sidekick of Sgt. Preston of the Yukon. "Here, King, here, boy." I want to be a Mountie in a red tunic and rescue half-frozen women. Another King is Sky King and his niece Penny. She wears a full skirt and ankle socks and penny loafers. They fly in to save the day and then fly out again like modest angels. Sky King waggles his wings as they depart and the people on the ground wave back in delight and admiration and eternal gratitude. Maybe he's related to the Flying Doctor, who ministers to the ailments of the Australian Outback, tends to snake-bite and fever and childbirth and madness. Maybe even does a c-section on a ewe whose lamb is breached. Then he washes off the gore and takes to the heavens on the way to his next emergency.

There is Saturday night, the special night, Hockey Night in Canada. The game comes on at nine. Our values are so warped, we hope there have been many fights in the first period, lots of whistles. That way we get to see all the second and third periods. On this night we get treats in front of the TV, a six-ounce coke and a bag of chips that we drown in vinegar until the chips turn to mush and we scoop the tangy pulp into our mouths by our fingertips, then drink what vinegar remains and wash it down with an ounce or two of Coke set aside for that very purpose.

After hockey, if time permits, there is Our Pet, Juliette. She has a big chest and blond hair and a lovely voice. My mom knits patiently through hockey to see her. Juliette has special guests like Robert Goulet, who sings duets with her. My mother gets frustrated if the games run past 10:30 and Juliet is truncated. The poor woman must feel like the step-sister elbowed aside by rough and tumble siblings Tim Horton and Bobby Baun. But Bobby Baun plays on a broken leg. Could Juliet do that? Can she hip-check someone into a stunned heap like Horton? Can she skate like Rocket Richard, ignite a crowd to screams as she carries an opponent on her back towards a paralyzed goalie who watches helplessly as the puck slips by? I doubt it. So she stays where she is, fighting for scraps of musical time left by brutal, sweaty, scarred men who exit the ice to drink beer, smoke cigars and scratch their privates. I don't know if TV goes on past that. My brother and I take our empty chip bag and pop bottle to the kitchen, brush our teeth, crawl into bed. Where we dream of being famous hockey players. We do not ever, not even once, dream of being Robert Goulet.

AGE OF INNOCENCE

Nobody locks their doors. I mean nobody. Some doors don't even have locks. Or if they do it has been so long since they were used, they are seized. People go away for two weeks and leave their houses open. That's just the way it is. Tourists might lock their cottages, but not locals. No one local steals from other locals. An unwritten rule.

Until *that family* comes to town. F*rom the city*. They must think they have died and gone to heaven. Every night, people put money and a note out in an empty milk bottle on the front step. *And leave it there.* The next morning the milk man, announced by the clip clop of Ned, the white cart horse, walks up to their doors, reads the note asking for two quarts of cream-top, a quart of chocolate and a pint of whipping cream. He'll shake the money out and replace the empty bottles with full; then he'll join Ned, already waiting at the next house. Ned has the route memorized.

One morning half the town awakes to no fresh milk. Someone has, once sleep settled over the work-weary, made a killing going door to door, pilfering the milk money. Scandalous! The operators at the telephone exchange develop stiff fingers from connecting all the calls that heat up the lines. Neighbour to neighbour, customer to dairy, aggrieved to police. Still, people are loathe to distrust and to change, so the next night, out go the money and notes in the empty bottles. Next morning, more disappointment, more cereal without cream, more black coffee.

Still, people refuse to believe this can be happening in this little town. Maybe someplace bigger, but here? Never! They once again trust their money to the night. This time the Chief of Police decides to go for a midnight stroll. Much to the chagrin of the money scoopers, who are bravely and blithely plundering. They are the glutted foxes in the henhouse, so satiated they don't hear the farmer coming. By sunrise everybody in town knows who the thieves are. Of course. Newcomers. From the big city. *Tan their asses*, is the consensus. *Make them pay it all back*. Except the three brothers have already spent all the two nights' loot. On candy. On baseball cards. On cigarettes. No delayed gratification for them, these pioneers of consumerism. And the family is too poor to cover it. So in recompense the thieves have to go around to each and every house they've stolen from and apologize.

They all have brush-cuts and impetigo and blue eyes. They have snotty noses and their clothes are ratty. One is tall and ferrety. He won't make eye contact. One is moon-faced, all forehead and round eyes. One of them has a speech impediment. As the story goes, he jumped off a school swing with his tongue between his teeth, landed so hard his knees came up to his chin, and, *snick*, lopped off his tongue-tip. When it's his turn to make amends to us he says, "Aggggh horrry." I laugh. He lowers his eyes. My mother cuffs me, causing me to bite my tongue. I taste blood, tinny and shameful. I notice that a single tear is trailing down his dirty cheek. I turn away, pretend I don't see, leave him at least that dignity.

The next week, it happens again. As before, the culprits are nabbed. But horror of horrors, they are local kids this time. Nobody has ever contemplated stealing that milk money before. It's as if it were invisible. Then the city boys helped the town kids to see it. They were optometrists, providing a clear vision of things as they were, not as they ought to be. Look at this chart. Read the first line to me: O P P O R T U N I T Y.

Kids, and not just kids, begin to think about unlocked doors and milk money and unsupervised store shelves and cars with keys in the ignition and purses on beach towels, possessions naively left for the taking.

A month later I go to visit my friend who lives above the bank. I lean my bike against the fence. We play table top hockey for two hours. My Montreal Canadians defeat his Detroit Red Wings in the best 13 of 25 games. Then I leave to go home for supper, only to find that the length of fence is bikeless. My first and only bike, the one I turned the handlebars backwards and up on, so they look like a bull's horns, so they look cool. Second-hand, but still, my first bike. It is found, halfway to Southampton on the road to Miramachi Bay, undamaged except for a flat tire. But still.

My mother says that from now on I should put it inside my friend's fence and close the gate. *Just to be sure.* The Dairy announces that from July on it will still deliver milk but that it will keep accounts that can be paid at the end of the month. *Please, do not leave cash payment in the bottles.* The older people around town grumble that we ought not to give in to moral decay. But I am the grandson of a dentist. I know about decay. It starts in one tooth, then next thing you know, another tooth deteriorates. Soon you have a mouth full of rot. My dad installs locks on the front and back doors both. Reluctantly but resignedly, I learn about keys.

Roger and his mother at Presbyterian Church Confirmation, 1962.

FREE WILL

"And what do you think of all this?"

Huh? I am rudely jolted back to the now. I was looking at the red-haired girl across the table, wondering how difficult it would be in the back seat of a car on a dark night to get all those buttons undone on that cashmere sweater, and what treasures might lie underneath were I able to do so. The Reverend is staring expectantly at me, the others await my response. We are seated on hard chairs around a long scarred table in the basement of the church. We are the Young People's Study Group and we gather here somewhat reluctantly each Sunday night to discuss Scripture. Well, I know I am reluctant. I don't want to miss Ed Sullivan and part of Bonanza to sit in this drafty basement and have my soul shrivel under the Reverend's gaze.

"No opinion at all? You usually have something pithy to say." We all pick up the venom in the Reverend's voice. He has silver metal-rimmed glasses accentuating sharp blue eyes, which are like knives at moments like this. Things have been slowly souring between us lately, since the day in his study at the manse six months ago when he asked me to kneel with him and pray, and I told him I didn't feel like it. How could I? His wife was out in the kitchen banging pots and getting a cake ready, a dog was barking across the street, I had to piss, my friends were at the beach waiting for me. Besides, how lame was that, kneeling with this old guy in the emptiness and pretending. He took that badly, phoned my mother to tell her he feared for my spirituality. Now she is on my case. That is why I'm here.

"Let me repeat: do you think humans deserve the free will God gave them? Haven't they misused it?" He taps a pencil eraser against his teeth. Okay, if he wants to spar, we'll spar. "Do we have free will?" "Of course. God bestowed it upon Adam and Eve, and Eve chose to sin by eating of the Forbidden Fruit; Adam abetted her. They exercised their freedom of choice and then God cast them out."

"So God didn't know they'd eat that fruit?" "I don't quite understand." "You have stressed that God is omniscient, right?" "Right." "He knows all?" "Yes." "All that has happened, all that will happen?" "He does indeed." "So he knew they'd sin." "Well, yes." "Then they had no free will." The other Young People begin to shift like cattle smelling a coyote. These evenings are meant to pass blandly into oblivion; this one is threatening to turn to pus. "If God knows every single thing that will happen to me, from what I will get on Chicky's physics test tomorrow to what I will have for breakfast on next Tuesday morning to what socks I will wear on February 28th 2000, then I have no choice. It is pre-ordained. Set in stone."

The Reverend's face is turning to stone. The temperature in the basement has dropped. Sweater Girl has her arms folded across her breasts. I briefly consider the possibility of erect nipples, and I'd linger there, but the Reverend brings me back to the fray. "You are mistaken. God will let you do as you wish. Should you choose not to study at all for that physics test and get 40%, he will allow it. Should you choose to study hard, and receive 90%, that too will he allow." "But does he know what mark I will get? Is he omniscient? He either is or he isn't." His mouth is a slit. "He is." "Then my mark exists now and nothing I can do will change it. Whether I study or not is foretold, my actions or lack of are sitting there in the expanse of his mind and they simply are. There is no *might be*, and without a *might be*, there is NO CHOICE!" I don't know how I came to be yelling, but I am. I feel as hollow and misplaced as I did the day a year ago when he placed the wafer upon my tongue at my confirmation, and how dry and unpromising it tasted. And then I go too far. "He gave Adam and Eve NO CHOICE. He forced them to sin. God is responsible for First Sin, and he was the one who should have been kicked out of the Garden, not poor Adam and Eve who were just God's two stupid marionettes."

What I have said is percolating through the layers of obedience and submissiveness that the other Young People have cultivated, and it is getting close to their hearts; when it does, they may burst. I don't want to be responsible for that. I know what I must do. The Reverend is searching for something suitable to say, but I am too quick. I stand, shrug my coat on, shove my chair back. "Sorry, Reverend, sorry all of you, but I can't believe any more in any god who uses me as a puppet. I am exercising my free will and going home." I stomp into my overshoes and add, as a parting slap, "to watch Bonanza."

The air outside the church is bracing, the night Sunday-still. I can see a trillion stars and more. My legs feel weak at first, a bit like a colt taking its first steps, but then I hit my stride; I gladly leave behind the Lord's House knowing my own house isn't far away.

"Back already?" asks my mom. "Yes," I say, "things broke up early tonight." I will deal with the following Sundays and her worry about my eternal soul later. Right now the map is burning and the Cartwrights are galloping across the screen. Adam will get shot, but live. Big Hoss will clumsily fall in love, but it will be unrequited. Little Joe, the hot-head, will use his fists to settle a dispute, then feel sorry afterward. Ben, Pa, the patriarch, will do his best to control his unruly children and to tame the Wild West, but he will realize that he really has no way to do that, and he's too old and lacks the will to anyway. He'll smile, beneficently, and sit back, and watch it all happen, the way he sort of knew it would.

KNIVES

All boys have knives. They might be born with them for all I know. I have a Hopalong Cassidy model, a sheath knife with an imitation mother-of-pearl handle and Hoppy's picture emblazoned on it. People envy it. I am offered many things in trade: marbles, BB guns, baseball cards, even, once, a puppy. But I will have no truck with trading my knife. I sometimes wear it on my gun belt. I have wild Bill Hickock twin six-shooters. The holsters are leather, studded with red gemstones, the pistols silver with, fittingly, fake mother-of-pearl handles. I am nothing if not co-ordinated. I practise in the mirror and get very fast on the draw. I know the guns aren't real, but the knife is, very real, very sharp. My grandfather hones its six-inch blade with his whetstone. My grandmother tsks and says he is irresponsible. He ignores her, keeps honing. He knows a dull knife is more dangerous than a sharp one.

One Friday after school, my brother and I are killing Indians. I have nothing personal against Indians. Our victims are not the nice Indians who live a few miles away, two of whom work for my dad. These are the non-Tontos, the whoopers on pintos who menace my heroes weekly at the cinema and on the radio and TV. Who tie US Cavalry soldiers soaked in honey over an anthill. An acquaintance, who also owns the garage and car dealership downtown, and for whom my dad has done renovations, has donated a flat pressed board GMAC Scotsman to our Wild West pageant. Although the squat Scot doesn't look Indian, he can be made one if you scream and squint as you throw yourself at him. He can be made Japanese or German if you are playing World War II. He is adaptable, this two-dimensional villain.

Our front lawn has two tiers. We are on the upper, the Scot, on the lower. He is passing by on his pony; I pounce, growling. I believe I see his startled face rise towards me. He knows he is going to the Happy Hunting Ground. Then the wind gusts him away from me and my Hoppy knife plunges flat against his chest and deflects down his pressboard thorax into my thigh. My howl turns to a groan. This movie has gotten too painfully real. I limp into the house, the knife still firmly imbedded in my flesh, just above the inner knee, the mother-of-pearl haft iridescent in the sun.

My mother is not sympathetic. She is preserving peaches and thus has no time for such interruptions. She sets me on the counter of the steamy kitchen, a cigarette dangling from her lips, sweat dripping from her chin, yanks the knife from my leg so quickly the pain dazzles me to tears. She gets down the bottle of rubbing alcohol from the cupboard above the fridge, pours it liberally on the wound. Oh it burns! She tapes a big piece of gauze over that, wipes my snotty face none too gently with a steam-soaked tea towel, sets me firmly down, tells me get out of her way. My leg is on fire. The Indians, those clever foes, have won.

It's Friday night; the stores are all open and it is our tradition to walk downtown as a family and meet and greet. I try to beg off; I want to lie on the couch and hurt in solitude. My mother will hear none of it. She puts fresh shorts and a shirt on me, and drags me downtown. Every second step is *STAB! STAB! STAB!* but her grip on my hand is unrelenting. If I want to play with knives I must bear the consequences. The next day my dad burns the GMAC Scotsman on the garden pile. I clean the blood off Hoppy and sheath him for good. I go back to practising my draw in the mirror. I like what I see there better. As the scar heals, it becomes round, white. I tell people it is a bullet hole. I got it the night I killed six men on the streets of Tombstone.

Roger's father, Bob Bell, on rock in Snake Creek,
just below the Bell farm.

OUT TO THE COUNTRY

I cling savagely to my father's pants, wrap my legs around his right leg. I screech. He drags me clumsily along. In the crook of one arm is his .22 rifle; cradled in the other, Fluffy, our cat. He is taking her *out to the country*. That means that she won't be back. She is old, very sick, but I want to keep her nonetheless. She is the only cat I have had in my five years. I beseech him, but he won't look down at me. He is purposeful and grim. If he looked down at me he'd falter and this task demands he not break. I want him to break. Oh please oh please oh please!

He stops, turns, looks over me to my mother. She stands near the side porch, smoking a cigarette and crying herself, gazing at but not really seeing her proud flower beds. "Bernice." When she turns her tear-streaked face to him, he nods down at me. She drops her cigarette, extinguishes it with the toe of her shoe, comes to us and gently tries to disengage me. I will not let go, I will not lose this battle. But finger by finger my hands are tugged from his pants. My mother wraps me up from behind in her arms the way she envelops me in a beach towel when I run to her from the waves of the lake.

Dad leans into the car and sets both cat and gun on the front seat, closes the door and turns back to us. Fluff begins a frail yowling, which saws into my chest. She knows. This is the cat who leapt onto the back of a stray lolloping hound that bounded through our back yard and nosed too close to her newborn kittens. She rode him yelping all the way to the alley before dismounting and trotting back to lick each kitten. This is the cat who bit the doctor on the ankle when he came to our house and gave me a needle that made me scream. This is my brave cat and she knows something is very wrong.

My dad kneels down to me. "Listen." I don't want to hear whatever he has to say, I lash out at him, but he gently catches my arms and holds them. "Listen," he repeats. I begin to subside, fatigue and defeat draining me. "She is very old and very sick. Her time has come. I'll be gentle, she won't suffer." He kisses me, rises, strides quickly to the car, starts it, backs out, drives up Market Street.

I let myself fall down. I weigh so much my mother cannot lift me. The earth is pulling me down and I lie there looking into the phlox along the garden edge, watching the busy ants. I lie there until my dad returns. He scoops me up as if I weighed less than a cat, carries me into the house, bathes me, puts me in my pyjamas and tucks me into bed.

The next day is Sunday. "We're going for a ride," announces my father, "just you and me." He drives the Mercury Monarch out to a side-road near my uncle's farm, stops the car."Let's get out," he suggests, and taking my hand, walks me up to a wild apple tree not far off the gravel. There is a patch of earth in the long soft grass that has been recently turned and tramped back down. "There is Fluffy's grave," he says. "I thought you'd want to see where I buried her. From now on, whenever we drive out this way, you can look at that tree and know she is there."

This gives me something to hold onto. I was afraid of *out to the country* because the country is so big, but this is close to town, we pass it all the time, I know where she is, I know she is someplace. I stand a moment longer. "Let's go home," I say. My dad nods.

We get another cat whom I grow to love. She too is named Fluffy. We have her many years. When she dies of some vague disease, I am old enough to do the burying. I tell my dad where and he drives me out to that same tree. My mother has wrapped her in a soft blue cloth. She is unbelievably heavy when I pick her up, as if gravity needs her badly. My father, former farm boy, who has known so many cats, buried so many, stands with his back to me, smoking and gazing out over the river valley below us, where the Saugeen works its slow way down to Lake Huron. I dig deep with the round-nosed shovel. The turned soil smells sweet. I lay Fluffy beside Fluffy, and it feels right. The hole fills back up easily.

Roger (left) and Jim on Dad's back at Goble's Grove, circa 1953.

COMMON DENOMINATOR

Roy's Confectionary is a name far too big for this little niche between the Five and Dime and the Chinese restaurant. It is a candy store which doubles as the catalogue order office too. As you enter, to your left are gleaming glass counters full of sugary choice. Straight back is a small counter, behind which is a curtain. My mother says they live back there, Roy and his wife. His wife has no name. My mother says she has ulcers on her legs and can barely move, poor woman. Once in a while, if you palm the bell on the counter, she will move heavily and painfully out from behind the curtain to hand over the parcel for your grandmother or your mother. She is a big woman in a shapeless salmon-coloured dress. Her hair is loosely done in a bun. Though she sometimes smiles, there seems to me little pleasure in what she does.

The pleasure is all Roy's, it must be, for what he dispenses is so much more enjoyable. I wonder if he knows his name is French for *king*? He is the King of Candyland, this big patient man who will spend forever with you while you order your daily fix. So much choice, so little money to mete out. Will it be wax lips or wax tubes filled with red sweet syrup? Once the syrup is gone, you chew the wax, a perverse pleasure which seems to disgust the girls. There are huge jawbreakers that distend your cheek, make you a facial Quasimodo. As they slowly dissolve, the colour changes, necessitating their frequent tongued expulsion so you can check calibre and colour. This too seems to repulse the girls. There are orange banana-shaped marshmallow treats, gumdrops, jujubes. There are candy cigarettes, with which we pretend to be our parents. They all smoke, so we will too. These treats are black with a frosted red and white tip. We puff, they glow hotly, we glow with sophistication. There is licorice, both whips and laces, both red and black. If you bite both ends off the whip you can use it as a drinking straw. The way to eat the laces is to tie them into a series of knots. You eat knot by knot. It is like prayer beads. You work your way along to heaven. Or you can use the whips to flail girls across the bare legs after they make fun of you.

What takes the time selecting is the mixing and matching. You attempt to maximize your total while covering all the bases. These are three for a cent, those five for two cents, those a cent each. You take two of the first. Roy puts them in the small paper sack and dutifully writes down 2/3 of a cent on a small pad of paper. You take four of the next; he plunks them into the bag, writes down 1 and 6/10 cents. You take two of the third; bagged and he writes 2 cents. *This* is where you learn fractions. Not in school. You have so far purchased 3 and 38/30, so 4 and 8/30, or 4 and 4/15 cents worth. You had five cents; therefore you have 11/15 of a cent left. You scan the counters, juggling figures in your head. Roy waits silently, as always. He will not rush us. Then, when you have made your final selections and you reach into your linty pocket for that nickel, your fingertips bump two coins. Your heart soars: you have a penny too; the process will continue. A lesser man than Roy might whimper, but he is too attuned to the universe to do that. Instead, he simply picks up his tongs, re-opens the paper bag, licks his pencil stub, nods for you to continue. Which you do, one painstaking fraction at a time.

FEVER

I am ablaze. I lie hazily on the couch in the living room, imagining that smoke is rising from my body. Although it is more likely it emanates from my mother, smoking nervously as she hovers nearby while the doctor examines me. "Stick out your tongue for me," he asks. I do. It feels thick and pulpy. "Wanna see?" he asks. I do. He holds a small mirror up. My tongue is white, covered in red dots, like a cake I had at a birthday party last month. When I am done looking, he sets the mirror down and gently tugs up my pyjama top, checks my armpits and inside my elbows. He pats my top back into place. He holds my hand up to my mother. "See the tiny bumps, how red the skin? Feels a bit like sandpaper. It's scarlet fever all right." His hands are cool, reassuring. His hair is very white, his eyes a summer-sky blue. He can go on holding my hand if he wants to.

My mother begins to cry quietly. It doesn't take much to make my mother cry. "She's a weeper," I've heard my Grandfather Bell say when my mom is sobbing about "poor Albert, what will he do without Florence?"

or about "poor Emma, how will she feed all those boys with Tom gone?" It's usually about death she cries, so I make the connection. "Am I going to die?" I ask Doctor Fraser, which pushes my mother deeper into tears. "No, no, just lie back and sleep." He smiles, puts that cool hand on my forehead, and I drift off.

When I awake, my dad is there in his work clothes, bits of sawdust still clinging to his skin. He is sitting beside me on the couch, looking down at me. There is a knock at the door. It is the doctor. "Bob," he says to my dad, "I have to quarantine the house. You'd better pack a suitcase before I do. Technically, you shouldn't leave, but you're the breadwinner so... I can give you five minutes. I'll take my time writing out this quarantine card."

"Where will you go?" my mom asks my dad, the unexpected refugee. "To your parents," he replies, then heads upstairs to gather what he needs, reappears quickly, sets down the suitcase. "I have some clean work shirts and pants on the line," says my mother, "don't leave until I get them for you. Mom will iron them for you." She hurries out, and Dad reaches down and picks me up, wraps me in his arms. He smells of sun and wood. "Be good for your mom," he whispers into my ear, "and get better. I'll come and see you." He kisses me, lays me gently back down, pulls a cover over me. Mom comes in with an armload of clothes. He hugs her, hard and long, takes the clothes, snatches up the suitcase and walks out the front door, which he leaves open. I feel a welcome wind push in. It soothes me. I see the doctor walk up and thumbtack a card to the front door. "Quarantine," it says in big red letters, "no entry." He smiles at my mother, swings shut the door, leaving me, my mom and my baby brother alone.

The next few days are fever days where everything drifts in and out: groceries left in a box on the front step; my grandparents saying something to me on the phone; radio; cold ginger ale, my mother tipping my head up so I can sip; red cherry jello, whipped, the way I like it; my dad outside, rapping on the window, waving and smiling.

Then my skin begins to peel off, like a snake's. I feel... fresh. One day the doctor appears, my dad right behind him, and, with great ceremony, the physician takes the card off the door, hands it to me. "Keep this as a souvenir," he says, laughing. While the three adults stand talking, I examine the card, as if its three words say all there is to say about these lost days. The thumbtack is still pushed through it; I test my fingertip against its point. It hurts a bit, but not much. I push harder, harder still, until it pops into me, the inner me. I stand and grin stupidly at the bright red dot welling against the formerly flawless skin, then I run outside to see what's the same and what has changed.

Roger and Jim on running board of stock car 203,
with driver Alex Steadman, circa 1955.

THRILLS AND SPILLS

My father comes downstairs dressed in his white coveralls. My mother has washed them and pressed them, and he looks dashing, the white contrasting with his sun-bronzed face and hands. He grins, picks up my brother and me as if we weigh nothing, carries us out to the car. Wednesday and Saturday, twice each week all summer long, we go to Bluewater Speedway, where he is the starter. He has a sawhorse with 5 holes drilled in it, which he puts in the trunk. For each of the holes there is a flag - green, white, checkered, yellow, red. He folds them carefully and puts them in the car trunk too. That sawhorse will stand beside him just below the announcer's booth, at hand, the flags ready to be pulled from their slots as needed.

The track is a raised and banked dirt one-third-mile oval on my uncle's farm. It has room for the cars and that is it. It has as its motto *Thrills and Spills* and there are plenty of those. People come from all over to sit on wooden planks nailed to sunken posts, all the way up the hill above the track. The hill is behind us, to the west, so the spectators aren't blinded by the setting sun. My favourite spot is above and to the left of the concession booth about half way up. Close enough to feel the rumble and smell the exhaust, high enough to see the whole track, watch the duelling that goes on. Sometimes a car rolls right off the track. Everyone holds his breath until the driver climbs out the window, waves up at us, then all applaud. Sometimes a car will lose a wheel; the car will dig to a stop in the clay, but the unleashed wheel will feel its oats, it will roll, roll, roll, off the track and across the apron and out into the parking lot, dinging parked cars as it goes, until the last ding makes it lose its will and it wobbles, then flops. There will be a stampede by those who left their cars there to see if they escaped damage or not. There will be laughter and relief among those who parked elsewhere.

I love these machines and the daring young men who pilot them. I sometimes get to sit in the cockpit on a driver's lap before the races begin. There is the Blue Pig, piloted by Rosey. Steady is behind the wheel of 203. Harvey Daniels from Tara drives #99, and the Nelson Brothers have a silver Pontiac, Big 6. There is Old Rye, and the sneaky fast Copperhead from Ridgetown. There are heats that lead up to the feature, a fifty-lap special. And the most exciting race of all, the one I almost pee my pants for when Hank Smith announces it over the loudspeakers in his silky voice, the Australian Pursuit. All the cars are on the track, and any car passed is out. When it comes down to two, jockeying, nudging, the tension is thick. Popcorn gets spilled, hot dogs are forgotten, cigarettes burn down and singe fingers.

The cars line up in pairs at the start line. My dad stands in front of them, like a matador, the bulls revving their engines impatiently. He crouches and the revving increases in pitch; my heart begins to thump. The whole world waits for my father. He holds the draped green flag aloft in his hand. The cars begin to move slowly by him, parting around him, re-joining up the track. Moses and his obedient Red Sea. He crouches down when they are all past him, lays the flag flat on the track. They round the far turn, approach expectantly, just held in check. Then he springs into the air, wildly waving the green as the cars leap from their tension and fly by him; he is in the middle of those charging cars and does not fear. When the last car clears him he sprints from the track. *The race is on.*

One evening, something goes wrong. Two cars rub as they greedily approach the start. They slither; more cars become involved. One flips, rolls right at my dad, raising a cloud of dust as it does so. Another car slides at where he was. My dad disappears in the melee. My mother drops her cigarette and her cup of Coke, leaps to her feet and runs down the hill, dragging my brother and me. She is crying, yelling out my father's name, gripping our hands so tightly we wince. Then the dust clears and there is my dad, intact, standing off to the side, his whites unbesmirched, his big grin dazzling. As if he has simply levitated out of harm's way. Mom lets us go and heaves a sigh, shakes her head, grins back at him, a grin that says *You are a fool and I love you for it.* He deftly produces the yellow caution flag, commands the growling stampede to a crawl while the flipped car is righted and shoved aside, the driver extracted unharmed. Then out comes the green again, slicing through the evening air. The sun sinks behind the hill and into the blue waters of the lake, lights come on, feet slam down on gas pedals and hands grip wheels, jaws clinch and eyes focus, revolution after revolution, a raucous gasoline beauty spilling over the farm fields and keeping resentful cattle from their appointed rest.

Four generations, circa summer 1951.
Left to right: Great-Grandmother Rushton;
her son Alban, Roger's grandfather, the dentist, holding Roger;
and his daughter Bernice, Roger's mother, holding Jim.

GREAT GRANDMOTHER'S EYES

My great-grandmother's eyes are blue, a vivid, mesmerizing blue, as if the summer sky has poured down and pooled there, to be magnified by the thick glasses she wears. Her eyes are most of her. The rest is wizened, doll-like. In the nursing home bed, though she is almost ninety years old, she is little more than a small child under the weight of the covers. They hold her down lest she float away. As if each year of her life on earth, instead of adding to her, diminishes her. If she lives to be a hundred, all that may remain will be a clear blue gaze framed by a halo of fine white hair. When we bring her to visit, my father lifts her in from the car as if she weighs nothing. He is strong, muscular from building houses, but he need not be to lift Great-Grandmother; she weighs little more than a sigh.

I go after school to visit her, although it frightens me to do so. I do not fear her, I do not fear this slow whittling away. But down the hall is a woman who screams things over and over. One day it will be, "Bring me ice-cold water from the deepest well." The next it will be, "My skin is on fire." Once I hear her yell, "I am a flaming comet and I shall ignite the heavens." My grandmother says, "She isn't right in the head, poor thing." I rush past the comet woman's room, followed by reaching hands of heat.

We talk of the world outside. She tells me of her youth, of dirt streets and horses and wagons, of a slower, more graceful, pace. She has a gentle voice that transports me back in time. She remembers the first flying machine she ever saw, of the noise it made, swooping in low over the fields outside town. The cattle stampeded and the milk was spoiled. A mare delivered a partly formed colt. She asks about space, is it true that they can now fly in space? How do they get up there, and stay there? How do they return? She says she imagines them as angels, with long languid wings, ascending towards God. I have been reading of Icarus, and I recite that story to her. "But his wings were man-made," she says, "of course he fell back. Angels wings grow smoothly and naturally from their backs, they can't fall off." "No wings," I say, "giant rocket ships to thunder skywards, then they fall back, like Icarus, leaving only a tiny explorer, that orbits, eventually splashes back down into the sea."

I tell her of Sputnik, how I went out to MacKinnons' farm, where it was darker, they had even shut out the yard light, and we stood out on their lawn and tipped our heads back and watched the Russian sphere pass brightly across the sky. We knew we were seeing something outside of our little lives. She asks me if it looked like a star. "It glowed, it did not glitter," I tell her. I don't tell her that it was all the myths I'd read: it was gold, it was silver, it was sun and moon and metal. It was Zeus' chariot, drawn by winged horses. Later still, I recount the stories of Yuri Gagarin and John Glenn, and she laughs like a little girl at the idea of men shoe-horned into tin cans and boosted into the sky to circle the earth in ever-diminishing orbits. She tells me, "I would like to circle the earth, see this little town from space, wave at those I love as I pass over. But," she says ruefully, "I don't suppose they'd take someone as old as I. No. But maybe you will do it for me."

One summer day she is not in her room; the covers are gone from the bed and there is no indentation on the mattress, as if no one has ever lain there; the house is silent, even the fire woman is quiet, her flames dampened. The lady who runs the place, grey-haired, red-faced, finds me standing lost in the doorway, kindly places her hand on my shoulder and tells me to go home, that my mother will want me, that Great-Grandmother passed on just hours ago and "is with the angels."

At the funeral two days later a very old woman stops in front of me, offers me her condolences. She stares hard into my face. "Young man, you have your great-grandmother's vivid blue eyes," she says. "Those were eyes that could see to forever and back." We bury my grampa's mother in Sanctuary Park, on the hill at the east edge of town, where you can get just a bit closer to the sky. That night, after supper at my grandparents' house, while dishes are being washed and cigarettes smoked, I slide out into the darkness and lie on the grass looking at all those stars. Somewhere up there she orbits. I can't see her, but I imagine her gliding on magnificent wings, those keen eyes searching me out. She is waving. I wave back.

Bell farm, Saugeen Township, late summer circa 1950.
First cousin Bob Bell holding Roger
and Grampa Bell (James) holding Bob's sister Barb.

HANDS

"Can you see him?" I shake my head, all I can see is knees, so my father places his large hands gently on my ribs and hoists me to his shoulder where I can look down upon his father, who seems to be floating on his back, eyes closed, upon a sea of white silk.

My grandfather's moustache has been trimmed; it is usually long and yellow and covers his mouth. Tea drips from it after he's raised his saucer to his mouth and slurped. It's a farmer thing to do, I have heard my dad say, though he doesn't do it and he was raised on the farm. My mom sometimes scolds my grampa, she can't understand why he won't drink from the fine bone china cups that look tiny in his big, gnarled paws. He just smiles at me, winks, takes a finger and wipes his moustache, ignoring the paper serviette my mom has folded and tucked under his plate. From up here I can see his lips, pinker than I imagined, his mouth straight, unsmiling.

He is wearing his black suit, the one he wears for special occasions.

This must be one, I guess, but I don't see sweets and teapots and tablecloths and that sort of thing. He usually wears the jacket unbuttoned, but now it is done up so I can't see if his gold pocket watch is in the vest fob. I love it when he picks me up and sets me on his knee and I ask him, "Can I hear your tock tick?" and he tugs out the heavy watch and holds it to my ear and I hear its metal heart beat. Then he helps me wind it, placing his big thumb and forefinger finger around mine, twisting new life into it. "Not too tight now," he warns. His suit prickles. Sometimes he'll place the watch face down on his kitchen table and take the back off so I can stare, mesmerized by the tiny toothed wheel rotating around a spring. My hands twitch then, I want to reach out and touch those fascinating innards. He won't let me, no matter how much I plead. "If you do, you'll break it, you'll stop time. We don't want to do that, do we?" And he hugs me to his chest. The suit prickles more, but I don't mind. I can sit here all day, we sometimes seem to, while we watch the little arm at the bottom zoom around the circle and the big hands move painfully slowly. He explains to me the I and V and X, and their combinations, he says when both hands are on XII, we will eat cucumber sandwiches with thick slabs of cheese and we will drink cold well-water.

His big rough hands are folded sedately on his belly. "Farmer's hands," I have heard my mother call them. I have seen them curled firmly around the handle of a pitchfork as he tosses hay for his Holsteins to gobble up or around an axe handle as he splits wood into pieces small enough to go into the cook stove where he bakes bread. I have seen them gentler on the teats of his cows as he coaxes milk out into a bucket. Once he beckoned me over, got me to squat down beside the udder, within the huge heat of the animal. "Open your mouth," he said, "and close your eyes." I did—and then a jet of something warm and rich filled my throat. My eyes shot open, I swallowed, coughed, he laughed and laughed.

"Lot better than from a bottle, all the goodness pasteurized out of it." I watched amazed as he tugged the long nipple in a different direction towards a nearby barn cat who gratefully licked it off the rough floor then sat grooming herself.

Whenever I go to visit him it is these big hands that dispense my favourite treat, Sultana cookies, but he and I refuse to call them that, they are *raisin cookies*, raisins flattened in sweet dough, layers of rectangles wrapped in cellophane that he slices open with a thumbnail. Each long layer is perforated and can be segmented into four. Sometimes, if he knows in advance that I am to visit, he'll hide a whole package, broken into individual pieces, between the logs piled in the woodshed just off the kitchen. The woodshed is dark, damp, has a dirt floor. I am a timid child, I cry a lot, have an over-active imagination. I hesitate, afraid to descend the three stairs into the gloom. He gives me a gentle nudge, stands behind me in the doorway, blocking some of the light. My greed drives me, I can already taste the to-be-found cookies as they crumble sweetly in my eager mouth. I slide my hand into one opening. Nothing, turn back to look at him. "Keep going," he says. Another gap, and my fingers find treasure; it dissolves in my mouth. "Don't stop now," he encourages, as my hand explores another crevasse, "there are more." Then, as my fingers touch something too soft for a Sultana, "unless the spiders or snakes have gobbled them up." I yank my hand out, scrape my knuckles, start to cry, and in a split second he is down the stairs beside me, kneeling, one arm around me, his other reaching into the woodpile and pulling cookie segments out like a magician pulling doves from a hat. Later, I sit in his lap in the rocking chair beside the ticking woodstove; I am shovelling in cookies, he is letting me eat the whole package, and I am still snivelling a bit, though I now know he was joking with me. I don't let go of tears easily; I almost take comfort in them. When I am full to bursting, he puts the watch against my ear, rocks us, and I drift off into a sugar-induced drowse.

I stare down at him, at how still he is. "Do you want to kiss him?" asks my dad. "No, but I want to touch him," so my dad helps me lean down to where I tentatively pat the blue knuckles and the veined back of his top hand where it rests upon the other. It is cold, unyielding, like the hand that slapped my mother one afternoon a year ago. I didn't know that man who thundered at my mom. "Jezebel," he roared at her. Why was he calling her that? Her name is Bernice. "Whore of Babylon. You are not fit to be this boy's mother." He put his arm around me, protectively, but I pulled away, ran to my mom. "What do you mean?" she asked him. "Women," he said, "all women are *strumpets!*" This last word he spat out distastefully, then he strode at her, nostrils flared and spittle on his lips, and his hand lashed out. I heard the flat smack of palm against cheek, saw her glasses sail across the room and land behind the Quebec heater.

She had stopped crying when my dad came home for supper. As she recounted what had happened, I saw violence grow purple in his face; he strode towards the living room, my mother tugging at his arm. His fist was balled up. "No," cried my mother, "no, Bob, he isn't himself, he's not in his right mind. He'd never have done that if he were." I clung to my dad's pant leg; it smelled of fresh-cut wood. My father slowed, looked at the old man, who was sedately sitting in the chair by the window, singing along with his favourite record.

Carry me back to old Virginny,
there's where the cotton and the corn and taters grow,
there's where the birds warble sweet in the springtime...

All the anger drained from my dad. He gingerly brushed my mom's swollen lips with a kiss, picked me up and tousled my hair. "We'll have to put him away," he said to my mom, "we can't take a chance now that this has happened." "Oh carry me back..." sang my Grampa Bell, his hands conducting some invisible orchestra.

This is the first time I have seen him since. "Your grampa's dead," says my dad. "Do you know what that means? It's sort of like he is sleeping." I lean down again and poke the back of his hand, but he doesn't stir. He isn't sleeping. I sense something more permanent. "It means no more tock tick." My dad's face is suddenly wet with tears; he pulls me to him tightly. I whisper into his ear, "And no more raisin cookies." "There will be raisin cookies," says my dad adamantly, "all the raisin cookies your belly can hold." And he is telling the truth. That night, back home, after sandwiches and tea and many people shaking hands with us, he and I sit eating Sultanas on the front porch. We have the door open and the record player on, and we play *Take me back to old Virginny* over and over again, while the warm June wind surges from the south and the taters and corn burst from the dark earth of my dad's big garden and the birds in the huge maple tree warble sweet.

Roger's parents, very dapper, circa 1947, in the Rushton back yard.

DAYS OF REST

Weekdays, the town vibrates with industry, people engaged at their work. My dad heads out early, drills and hammers, lifts walls, raises roofs. The days are never long enough, and in the evening he'll scan blueprints and sip rye. My Grandfather Rushton arises at 5 a.m., works on dentures in his lab, sees patients from 8 until 6. After supper, he may go back to the lab or tend to a late-comer who has lost a filling and can't wait until morning. My Uncle Jack, up at the *Biggest brush factory in the British Empire,* as the locals proudly proclaim it, twists straw around handles and wires it into place, inserts Mexican hurl into holes, feeds gnashing machines, Saturdays he goes out to check his trap-line. My mother and grandmother and Aunt Isobel cook endlessly for insatiable mouths, they dust, wax floors on their groaning knees, haul hot water for laundry, hang clothes on lines. My aunt styles hair in her kitchen, my mom sometimes works in a clothing store selling dresses and hats to the town's fashionable women.

But Sundays are different. People stop, things stop. Breathing seems to slow. A calm settles over the town. Breakfast is later. Sunday School and church, then off come the constraining ties and girdles. No normal store is open. The exception is in summer, when the town is full of tourists, the beach places are doing business, the Town Booth's churning out the world's best french fries in paper cones and the Tuck Shop is selling foot-long hot dogs mounded with relish and tomatoes and mustard and carrots and radishes. And farmers, of course, must feed their livestock, and dairy cattle must be drained twice a day. But mostly the town on Sunday says, "Enough is enough. Give me a break." People pursue leisure activities. A bit of gardening, some fishing, reading under a tree. They stroll, go to the beach. They do not work and they do not shop.

Sundays we go out to my country aunt's house and while the adults sit and talk, my cousins and my brothers and I head to the barn and climb up into the mow or stare at the sow that ate her farrow, or sit on the idle tractor imagining we are driving. We sometimes step in shit and have to get cleaned off by our mothers. We make home-made ice cream from fresh cold rich cream, milked and separated that morning. We have a huge supper and groan away from the table, regretting that third slice of pie.

Or my parents and my brothers and my town aunt and uncle and their kids wedge ourselves into a big Pontiac and drive all over Bruce County, Tobermorey to Kincardine, on paved roads or gravel roads or dirt roads that are barely more than cow paths. There is never a destination. Gas is cheap and the day is endless. My dad and uncle drive by memory and by feel. Once we get lost outside near Cape Croker, driving in circles as the sun drops, my mother chewing away at my red-faced father and my aunt at my grim-lipped uncle up front, blaming them for getting us to "wherever in the hell we are" and trying to keep all the hungry kids in the car allayed with handfuls of Pink Elephant Popcorn and warm Coke. And the relief when we finally break out and find Wiarton, hit the only restaurant still open, tie into wads of greasy fries and battered fish.

Christmas is like a bunch of Sundays crammed together. Businesses try to shut down early Christmas Eve. Late-minute shoppers are tolerated but shooed out store doors brusquely. The denizens of the pool hall have laid down their cues; the felt has been swept, the long fluorescent lights turned off, the Boston and snooker balls have been racked into their orderly triangles. Even the beverage rooms eject their tipsy patrons who uncertainly make their way home. The gifts are all bought and wrapped, trees trimmed. Darkness falls and lights come on, windows steam up. Nothing is open; no merchant will re-open for at least three days. What you don't have you won't have. Unless it snows heavily, the plows will stay parked. Unless there is a fire, announced by the siren over the town hall, the volunteers won't budge. The cop shop is closed. There is a hush and it is proper.

This all changes with the variety store. Here we have known no such creature. I do vaguely remember once staying with my Toronto aunt and uncle. Sunday morning, the house still, my brother and I were taken by my dad for a long walk to let the sleepers sleep, and on that walk we saw busy roads, streams of traffic. On Sunday! And we came across a small store, *open*! It amazed me that somewhere there were stores open that day of rest, that my dad could buy cigarettes and we could buy hockey cards and wax lips full of syrup. And now our town is to have such a store, right up the alley from our place in what used to be a service station. It will be open 7 to 11. It will be open Sunday. It will sell groceries too, fresh meat and bananas and potatoes, tinned goods, frozen foods. My mother vituperates against it, says it is unnecessary and only the lazy will patronize it. Church pulpits sermonize against it: it is sinful, it's a tear in the fabric of the Sabbath.

But six months after it opens, the parking lot is always full. My mother begins to shop there, *for convenience*, she claims. When news leaks out that it will open Christmas Day, from noon to four, the town is scandalized. This is going too far; its staff refuses to work that day, but the owner has his family tend the till and stock the shelves, and people remember that they needed whipping cream or tinned corn to go with the turkey or a cabbage to make coleslaw or that they don't have enough stale bread to make stuffing. They don't mob the place but enough trickle shamefacedly in and out, and others begin to wonder what the fuss was, and soon other merchants must rethink. If they are closed and business is to be had, they might as well have a piece of that action. Not Christmas, mind you, but longer hours, more days maybe. Worth considering. Nothing happens right away, but the seed is planted.

The next Christmas Day, my mother realizes she hasn't enough brown sugar to make the sauce for the carrot pudding, and I must leave my road hockey game to run up the alley to the variety store, get her a big bag. I find it on the shelf, carry it to the check-out, pay. All so easily done that I don't even notice what's lost in the doing.

BENCHED

My face burns. Sitting here, unnoticed. At the cold end of the bench, farthest from the gate I will never use. We pine-riders nick-name it Siberia. I am on the Bantam All-Stars team, but I am no All-Star, I should not be here. David belongs; oh man, he can skate. He is a figure skater too, so smooth he is almost frictionless, so strong. And Ron belongs, and Allan, and Murray; they are puck wizards, talented stick-handlers. I have never been good enough, and I know it. My feet don't work well when my skates are on. I'm wobbly, what they call a tripod, leaning on my stick to stay up. Even with that crutch, I fall a lot. I miss easy passes, even those right on the tape; when I return a pass it's often behind the intended recipient, who usually shakes his head in frustration. Nor can I shoot. Some people have a heavy shot, one that thuds against the goalie like a brick, one that hurts; some have a fast shot, a blur up under the crossbar. I have a floater. Goalies must smile when they see me set to shoot; they have time to file their nails, or write a letter home before my puck gets there.

I first realized how pathetic I am a few years ago in Pee Wee House League when the coach of the PeeWee All-Stars came to the house one winter night after supper. From where I was reading in the living room, I heard him tell my mom they needed players. My heart jumped. Was it possible? I was ready, oh I was ready. Then he continued, asked if my younger brother Jim, who was in a lower age group, Squirts, could *move up* to the Pee Wees. He was good, the best maybe, and they needed him, *really* needed him. I quietly closed my book, slid off the couch, went into the living room coat closet under the stairs, pulled the door shut behind me, slumped down among the Eatons catelogues, and let the hot tears gush. *He's two years younger. Not fair not fair not fair!* The vacuum cleaner beside me offered no consolation. Nor did the coats, scarves, hats, mitts, boots, old magazines, photo albums. After the coach had left, with my parents' approval, my mother found me weeping. She tugged me up and out of that closet, sat me down with her arm around me, tried to tell me that I had no reason to cry, that I was better than Jim in school, my marks were tops in the class, that not everyone is good at everything. But given the choice of being good at hockey or school, who wouldn't choose hockey?

Now, four years later, here I am: bigger, but no better. The only reason I'm on the All-Star team is that there were no try-outs, there aren't enough guys in this town of this age who play hockey. I have succeeded by default. I seldom play; I dress, sure, but I *ride the pine*, exiled. Even in scrimmages at practice, I ride the pine. After the best game of my life, in Paisley, a village near here, due to a player shortage and the fact it was an exhibition game, I got to play a regular shift and scored a hat trick, though I wasn't deluded, none of the goals was pretty, one scooped in as I sat on my ass in the crease. Next game, when it counted in the standings, I rode the pine. Beside me, equally ignored, sits Brian, who may be too small and who hates contact, and Terry, the spare goalie, who dresses as a skater when he isn't tending net.

Tonight we have come by bus all the way to Elora, the final game of the Western Ontario Championship. Some of our parents have come to cheer us on. The atmosphere on the bus was festive on the way down but it is no longer. We are losing 5-2 with only five minutes remaining. This is it, the last game of the year, my last game of Bantam. I stare at the two coaches, trying to bore this into their brains. *Hear my plea. The game is lost anyway, let me on the ice, just once, in front of my mom and dad. Let me say that I played in a championship game.* And one of them actually looks at me, as if he has heard me. He glances up at the clock, back at me, turns and whispers something to the other coach – who looks down at me for a long, long time, then shakes his head, goes back to watching the ice. My face is on fire. I am afraid I will cry, so I put my head down, way down between my knees, and for the rest of the game, until the final bell ends the misery, I stare accusingly and fixedly at my skate blades, which don't have a single drop of snow on them. As if I weren't even there.

IOOF Pee Wee House League team, circa 1958.
Roger, middle row, far right, eyes closed.

BURN 3

Her hands are insistent upon my shoulders, her voice urging me back from a snug place I want to stay curled into. I shrug up, rub my face, she pulls open the curtains at the foot of the bed. "Look." I crawl forward on hands and knees, lean on the windowsill, feel its chill shock my palms. My eyes aren't yet fully working but they suffice: the sky to the east is bright and lurid orange. I look up at Mom. "The arena is on fire," she says. This jolts me up, my bare feet find themselves cold against the linoleum. "You must have been sleeping soundly. The siren went and went. Your dad's already up there." My dad the volunteer fire fighter, called from dinner, from dancing, from Sundays with guests, from warm beds in the deep dark winter night.

The alarm clock registers 4 a.m. Only three hours ago I was in the arena, packed in with all those rabid others, as the Junior game, the seventh and final one, went into overtime, double, triple, on and on. No one, it seemed, would ever score; the goalies, slugging all that wet and heavy equipment, seemed implacable, unwilting in their creases. Every rush that came at them was repelled. Until, at almost 1 a.m., well past all of our bedtimes, Ross, a crew-cut local boy, lifted his own rebound over sprawled defenders and a frantic lunging goalie, pushed the twine far back, pushed the roar of the ecstatic crowd high into the thick air and he was lifted on the shoulders of his teammates and carried around the ice to our adulation and then the cup was presented and the crowd surged out the doors and home to beds that they tumbled into smiling.

And now I'm back, my brother beside me, in our snowsuits, which we don't really need, so intense is the heat. My forehead and cheeks tighten, the way they do at the beach, the summer sun on my face. We are standing kitty-corner from the arena, from where my father and the others are shadows from the underworld futilely trying to douse the madness raging there. The arena is all wood and the fire loves it, licks it avidly. So vehement are the flames that the asphalt shingle exterior of the Legion Hall across the road begins to bubble and melt like a slice of cheese in an iron frying pan.

I lean back against the legs of my mother, who is holding my baby brother. Someone nearby says, "Musta been a cigarette, musta been, somebody didn't stub out a butt. All that wood..." Does it matter how it started? With the centre of the world on fire? I watch with bright eyes as the whole building aches against the heat, I feel it roasting me, a turkey in a hot oven, and then some faceless fireman runs across the road, the others following, yelling, "Move back, move back NOW, the roof!" And the roof, suddenly tired, like those sagging defensemen and goalie hours ago, gives up the battle and collapses, spraying cinders up like fireworks, rolling a tsunami of heat out over us and down the streets of our little town, melting snow, melting the night right into reluctant morning, where my soot-faced father slumps at the kitchen table, staring at the coffee cup he cradles in his stained hands, knowing that he must soon go to work, that the day is merciless and waits for no working man, no matter that he is dog-tired and his skin singed, no matter that he spent the too-short night giving all he had.

COOL 3

Linda has found out I am going to Toronto, to an army surplus store. If she gives me the money, will I buy her an army shirt, size small? "Army stuff is sooooo cool," she says. She has that look in her green eyes, the look that makes me melt. Of course I will, of course. And I do, I return Monday with it and when I hand it to her she squeals in delight and she hugs me so hard my spine turns to liquid fire and I can't even breathe or move from the spot until she has been gone five minutes.

She takes my breath away again the next day, for a different reason. She has sewn shut the side vents of the shirt and is wearing it as a minidress. Emphasis on the mini. Those legs. Those smooth brown exposed legs. This is too much. I spend most of each day hunched over trying not to think of something sexual. Baseball. Algebra. Dental floss. "How do you like it?" she says. Spins around with her arms spread so it rides even higher. Oh, Jesus, don't do that. "Love it," is all I can croak. "*Love* it." The energy it would take to say more has all rushed to my loins. Besides, what else is there to say?

But the principal scowling down the hall towards us clearly doesn't love it. For weeks now he has been measuring skirt lengths, sending home girl after girl, raging over the PA system about morals and standards. He sends the wayward girls to their negligent parents, the sinners come back; home, back, home, back. Until the offending hem falls within the bounds of decency. He hauls Linda away from my lecherous eyes, sends her all the way out into the country where she lives.

Back she comes with the same dress on the next day, a defiant smile on her face. And back home she goes. This has become a siege of sorts, a moral erosion. Will the walls of decency hold, or will the shameless harlots' indecency wear them down?

I, personally, favour indecency. I support girls in minis sitting up on lab stools with bare legs clasped because I know that sooner or later their vigilance will waver and they will unclasp, they will slowly uncross those legs to re-cross them. They will drop a pencil and bend down to pick it up. They will walk up the stairs ahead of me between classes. I am a normal, healthy boy so I am in favour of all exposed female flesh. Yes, I applaud their rebellious embrace of fashion-cool, but it is a self-serving applause, a drooling applause.

In Latin we are studying the Olympic motto: Citius. Altius. Fortius. Faster. Higher. Stronger. I have committed it to memory, and I repeat it aloud as I wander this wonderland of thighs and their environs. I emphasize the *Altius.*

HAZEL

I awake several times during the night to wind clamouring and rain smacking hard against the wall beside my bed, but I manage always to find wherever I was in my dream and regain it, as if my dreams are the cliff-hangers I go to see each Saturday at the show. Finally, about 4 a.m., curious about how long this is lasting, I get up; since I'm older I get to sleep on the outside of the bed, thus I don't wake my brother Jim when I climb out. Good, I don't want him following me around asking questions. His mouth is half open, he is snoring lightly, as he always does; the doctor says he has excess bone in his nose; and he sticks things up it too, so no wonder. Mom had to take him to Dr. Fraser to get pussy willows out last spring. His right arm hangs awkwardly behind his back. I wonder what he is dreaming, if he and I, because we sleep side by side, ever dream the same thing. I pad across the hall outside the bathroom and into my parents' bedroom, past their slumbering forms, peer out the front window. The big maple tree is thrashing unhappily in the rainy nimbus of the streetlight in front of Mr. Semple's house. I go downstairs, through the kitchen and into the living room, which has three tall windows. Rain hammers against all of them at once, and I can see what looks like a small river running down Market Street. I will be six in three months and I have not yet seen a storm like this. Snowstorms, yes, our town gets huge ones every winter, they come barrelling in off the lake and often the whole town shuts down in deference to their power. But this isn't soft, this isn't muting things the way big snow does. There is an anger to this, a bullying, a desire to break things, the way last fall some friends and I threw rocks through windows of the old empty house down the street. I lose myself staring out the window; I have heard the word *banshee* from my mother; I don't know exactly what it means, but this must be close. I have been watching the world tear itself to pieces for I don't know how long when I feel my dad's hand on my shoulder. He doesn't say anything; we just stand in our pyjamas and watch branches snap and fly, water gush. He swings my grampa's rocking chair around so it faces the window, sits down and pulls me up into his lap. I like the way he smells, of wood shavings and cigarettes. I lie back against him and he begins to rock. The next thing I know it's morning, grey and dull, still windy but no longer shrieking, and I am back in bed with my brother, who is sitting up and rubbing his eyes.

We can smell bacon and eggs and coffee and stumble downstairs to the big kitchen, where my dad is sitting at the table sopping up egg yolk with his toast and my mom is cooking. They are both soberly listening to the radio. As we eat they explain to us that Hurricane Hazel went through last night, that there was a lot of damage, that people were killed in Toronto, drowned when their houses were swept away. The phone rings, it's my uncle. Does my dad want to go with him to Southampton to see the big locomotive that tipped over when the tracks washed out? Of course, and I get to go with them. All up Highway 21, where there used to be farm fields there are miniature lakes and I stare out the window at big trees ripped root-first out of the ground. We sit in the car in Southampton and watch huge yellow cranes slowly right the black locomotive, which looks just like the one in my train set. There are knots of people everywhere, talking and pointing. The progress seems too slow and I ask my dad why. "It's very very heavy," he says. I don't really understand heavy, I can lift my toy locomotive easily back onto the tracks when it derails.

My dad and uncle are growing tired of this, and I am too. "Should we check the house?" asks my uncle Jack. They mean their dad's house, my Grampa's house. He died last June and the old log house has sat empty since. Ten minutes later we are crossing the one-lane bridge over the Saugeen River. The water beneath is ugly, brown and full of debris, and it is higher than I have ever seen it. It is up near the barn at Harry Thede's farm. I have seen it there in spring before, when the river comes unstuck and big slabs of ice thump down towards the lake, but never in fall. Just after the bridge the car slows and turns on the concession road where it dips then rises towards the family farm. But Jack stops. Snake Creek is in the way, *really* in the way. It is normally placid, little more than a stream, maybe three feet deep, meandering down to the much bigger and hungrier Saugeen. Every summer my dad takes Jim and me to fish off the big rock near the bridge. He hoists us onto his shoulders and wades out. We pull in baskets of chub and shiners, which dad buries at the base of his tomato plants. It is normally a lazy creek. Not today; today it is rushing high and cold over the little bridge, maybe two, maybe three feet above the roadway, as if it's in a hurry to be part of the river.

They silently examine the situation, then my uncle opens the trunk of his car. He has a long rope in there, and chest waders; he shuffles off his shoes, climbs in to the chest waders, takes one end of the rope and ties it around his waist, goes to the front of the car and ties the other end to the car's chrome bumper. He slowly advances down the slope to the bridge while my dad plays the length out through his calloused hands. Uncle Jack grips the bridge railing hard and begins his way across. I can see that the water is very strong, and greedy too, it wants to pull my uncle off his feet and take him out to the lake with it. My uncle leans as he steps, the water grants him grudging progress; he is about half way across and looking like he might make it when the water seems to rise right to his armpits, boils up around him as if he were a rock. I see the strain in his back and shoulders as he fights the current, every step an effort, soon the road begins to slope up, soon he's out of the worst. He pauses for a moment, to breathe maybe, or to flash some assurance at us, when he's tugged off the railing and he disappears into the grey rush. My breath stops. My dad plants his feet and puts everything he has into that rope, all his carpenter muscles, his baseball muscles, his garden muscles, he pulls handful after heavy handful of the rope to a sodden pile at his feet, in a frantic tug o' war. And up pops my uncle from out of that foaming torrent, like a fish my dad has hooked, and my dad pulls him back to us, lands him, and my uncle has that big sloppy grin all over his face. My dad has him now in his arms, and they are hugging, slapping one another on the back, both laughing. "My glasses," says Jack suddenly, reaching up with his hands to his dripping face. My dad shakes his head, as if to say *long gone*, they both look meditatively at the torrent. I imagine those black-framed glasses tumbling through that cold dark flood, landing on the face of some big lazy pike.

When we get back to my uncle's place, my mom and brother are there. "Where are your glasses, Jack?" asks my aunt. Like two boys caught in some misfired prank, they explain to their wives what they wanted to do and what went wrong; the women go pale, then their faces become grim. "Lucky fool," my aunt says to her husband. "Stupid buggers," my mom chides them. They deflect the admonitions, both keep grinning, the adrenaline rushing in them like the swollen creek. "Think about what you taught *him*," my mom says to them, pointing at me. My uncle winks at me. I copy their cocksure smirks, and she shakes her head, knowing I'm already lost to her.

My dad walks us home. I get out my train set, click together the big oval of track, plug in the transformer. I couple all the cars together. I set up the station, farmhouses, cattle yard, populate the small town with men, women, children, animals. I am God Almighty. I make a whistling noise with my mouth, tip over the two trees that stand by the station. One lands on the stationmaster and his little dog. The other flattens a cow grazing benignly nearby. I run the locomotive as fast as I can, and it spills going around the corner, right onto the stiff watchers, who are too close, and pay for their nearness. I get out my yellow metal crane and hoist the helpless turtled machine back onto the tracks. I spend the rest of the day playing Hazel, destroying and resurrecting, grinning like a stupid bugger, and dreaming of a happy-go-lucky bespectacled fish who sees things now the way my uncle does.

Roger as Toy Soldier, ready for Santa Claus Parade, 1961, outside Waterloo Street house; the other soldier is either Roger's mother or his brother Jim.

THE EVENING DESCENDS

I am doing circles on my trike on the sidewalk in front of the Church of the Latter Day Saints. I see two older boys, the blond and his darker friend, struggling down Market Street from the direction of the Mill Creek, carrying between them something large and heavy. I do a couple of figure eights just to show off for any passing spectators and move curiously up the street towards the blond boy's house.

They are staggering now, and as they get closer I can see they have a seine net twisted in their sweaty hands, the tendons and veins of their forearms bulging, and in the sagging middle of the seine, a huge snapping turtle is thrashing wildly. Straining, they halt, display it mid-air for me to have a look. It has age upon it, moss grows on its shell, and it has a heft beyond what a young turtle might have. It ceases frantic pawing and sways its head back and forth, seeking something on which to lock those brutish jaws. Its eyes are shiny black and tiny and filled with that primitive desire to maim. I stay well back, I've heard many stories of fingers and toes lost to such jaws in the murky creek water. Some bigger boys once snickeringly told my friends and me that a guy who was skinny dipping up there had his *thing* taken right off, as if it were a big fat worm dangling temptingly in front of the turtle. Now he has to sit down to pee.

The blond boy, keeping his end taut, twists the knob of the front door of his little house, leans in, keeping the tension on, and yells for his dad. His dad comes running, wearing slippers and gripping a section of newspaper in his hand. When he sees the turtle he stops dead, his face lights up. "She's a beauty, boys, a real beauty. Set her down, boys, careful now, set her down, but don't let the tension off."He picks a fallen tree branch from off the street edge, slides the thick end in through a small hole in the net, pokes at the turtle. It fluidly swivels its head and latches onto that branch; it must think it finally has one of its tormentors in range. The branch snaps easily, and I jump back. The man laughs, tucks the paper under his arm, rubs his hands together. "Boys, she must be 40 pounds; lots of soup there, lots of soup." My stomach lurches at this. His next words are like a punch in the chest. "Son," he says to the blond boy, "hand me that end, and fetch me the sledgehammer from the back shed."

I turn my tricycle for home, begin to pedal hard. Already at this age I have seen the slapstick blood-spraying runs of decapitated chickens, the sack full of unwanted barn kittens swung against the post with a pulpy thud, the flipping fish pinned through the shaft of a nail protruding from the cleaning table, then eviscerated with precision, the gutted deer hauled back feet first to the rafters before the sharp knives slide coolly between hides and flesh. I do not wish to witness the snapping turtle broken like an ancient rune crudely decoded. I speed home while the evening descends around me like the muddy brown water of the creek trying to fill my pumping lungs.

BEHIND THE HIGH HEDGE

I am filling in for Gib's Lad. Gib is the butcher and anyone who works for him, the least senior of the crew, is called *Gib's Lad* – slurred in our parlance into one word – *Gibslad.* Gib's Lad sweeps up blood-soaked sawdust and lays down fresh. He helps re-stock the shelves with cans and jars of mustard and sauerkraut and relish. He gets to put down the front awning to keep the sun out. Sometimes he gets to lean into the cold display case counter and array in an attractive manner freshly squeezed sausage ("like tiny, perfect linked turds" snickers one of the older boys) or newly sawn pork chops.

This afternoon of this perfect summer Saturday, I am pedalling a large, older bike with a big steel carrier mounted on the bars. In the carrier sits a waxed cardboard box and in that box, snugged in brown butcher paper held closed by elastic bands, nestle beef briskets and sirloin steak, chicken legs and breasts, soup bones and bacon. The briskets and sirloin go to Mrs. Muir, the chicken to Mrs. Kolb, the bacon and soup bone to

Miss Ruby. At each house I lean the bike against a tree or a lamppost, select a package and carry it to the front door, knock, wait, am greeted by name and a smile from someone I know. I hand over the meat, a gracious woman hands back money, wishes me a good afternoon, pushes the door shut. I re-mount the bike and continue my nearly mindless navigation of the streets.

The last package says *Beef Heart* and it is for a house I do not know, though I have passed it hundreds of times, as I have done with every other house in this little town. I think I have met every inhabitant of this place but I do not know those who live here. The house is surrounded by a high hedge; I am familiar only with its viney, overgrown upper storey, its steep metal roof with a lightning rod atop the chimney. I enter, as Gib instructed, via a creaky wire gate set into the hedge and rap at a door whose paint is scaling. The woman who greets me is dark and has her hair severely pulled back. She asks me simply how much, in an accent I cannot identify, goes off to get change. I step in. The kitchen is dim, its blinds drawn, and is very warm, a big old wood-fired cooker kicking out heat. On it, two large pots are boiling away, emitting a fleshy smell. At the table, a very old woman with a moustache and no teeth smiles gummily at me. Beside her a strange little man with pointy elf ears, big bright eyes and sharp little teeth is dipping toast strips into a decapitated egg. He inserts each strip, soaks it thoroughly in yolk, extracts it, raises it to his lips, licks the drooling yellow, then tips back his head and sucks each piece noisily down. The old lady is spooning thick clots of strawberry jam onto hunks of toast and gumming them in.

The first woman returns and drops a handful of coins into my palm. As she does so the little man rises from his chair and approaches me. He can't be more than four foot six. He is offering me something, a drooping piece of yolk-saturated toast. He gently puts his hand on my forearm and licks his lips. The yolk is congealing. The heat and the thick olfactory mix of jam and boiling meat begin to overwhelm me. I bolt out the door and through the gate. I don't bother to close it, just leap on the bike and hammer, sweat-slicked and nauseous, back to the cool oasis of the butcher shop.

It proves no relief. Carcasses are being hauled and knives are busy. The band saw zips effortlessly between ribs. Cleavers sever flesh and bone, thump into butcher blocks shining with gore. Something in that house has wormed into me, something unfamiliar. A wave of vertigo washes over me; I push open the back door, step out into the alley, vomit into sawdust I piled out here two hours ago. "Better go home," says Gib when I step back in wiping my swampy mouth. I skip supper, stay in my room. My mom visits me before she goes to bed. "Must be something you ate," she says. "It'll pass. Try to sleep."

I crave oblivion, so I do try, but my guts clench and my dreams roil with pointy teeth and ears, yolk hardening on unwashed plates and spoons, hearts boiling in open pots in someone's unnatural kitchen. The sun rises reddish-brown, greasy, smeared across the horizon. My mother brings me breakfast in bed, apple juice and toast with strawberry jam. The juice is cool, but one bite of the toast and my gorge rises; I shove aside the tray, rush to the toilet, puke and puke and puke some more. I am exhausted. My mother sympathetically washes my face and helps me back to bed. She feels my forehead. "You have no fever," she says. "Strange." If only she knew *how* strange.

Easter Sunday circa 1952 - Bernice, Jim and Roger
all spiffed up for church, front lawn of Market Street.

LETTUCE PRAY

I have always thought it strange. Where *is* the lettuce that the Reverend is asking to pray? Why would he be asking it to pray? How can it put its hands out and bow its head (it is all head) and talk to God? I wonder if he'll ever say "Carrots pray," or beets, or potatoes, or peas. Does he ever invoke prayer in the whole garden? Maybe he is trying to get my non-churchgoing Grandpa to pray. Grandpa says he hasn't been to church since he got married and has no intention of wasting a goddam good morning listening to some holier-than-thous telling him how to live. While we go off to the Presbyterian Church and my Grandma heads off to the United Church, Grandpa listens to the radio, maybe works in his lab, or polishes the car, or hoes his garden, which has glorious lettuce, because every time a rabbit comes in search of sustenance, he leans out the back door with his little .22 and blasts it. He keeps the Sabbath the way he keeps his garden, in his own way.

It isn't only praying vegetables that are strange about church. It is farmers that you never see dressed up except then in too-tight shirt collars, their ears red, sweat at their freshly barbered hairlines, as if their big and unnaturally hatless heads might explode from the pressure. It is fathers that have been out late Saturday night at the beverage room, staggering home down leafy and deserted streets, fumbling keys into shifting locks of front doors of dark houses, stairs that creak and sway as they less than successfully head up, and wives that roll coldly away from them as they fall into beds. You can tell them in church because they have on too much aftershave, which is unsuccessful at masking the waft of whiskey and draft beer. You can tell them because they nod and fall chin-first into fitful dreams about halfway through the sermon, only to be sharply brought back to hellfire and damnation by a vicious and unfeminine dig in the ribs.

Because hellfire and damnation is what the Reverend preaches. He is Scottish, right down to his name, and his Bible may as well have stopped at the end of Malachi, where God says, "For behold, the day cometh that shall burn as an oven; and all the proud, yea, all that do wickedly, shall be stubble; and the day that cometh shall burn them up." There is not an ounce of pity in the Reverend, I'm sure. We *are* stubble, especially our fathers, who art not in heaven nor ever shall be, for they are walking through the valley of the shadow of our mothers' hard looks.

My favourite Reverend day is the Day of the Two-Hour Sermon: it has been triggered by a perfume with the suggestive title, *My Sin*. The Reverend rants and he raves, he paces across the front, down the one aisle and back up the other; righteousness drips from his chin and his robes flow around him like deep blue flame. His eyes too are blue, steely blue, and when he fixes them upon an unfortunate member of the stubble, that person must avert his or her gaze or be turned to a pile of ashes. "What kind of a world is it," yells the preacher, "where sin is so easily accepted? Where women must anoint their bodies with such filth to attract men? Where commerce must employ Satan as a salesman?" Around and around and around he marches, his words of contempt and condemnation pattering down around us like the vitriolic spittle of a highly incensed volcano. "We're surely damned," says the Reverend, "if this is where we have arrived. Debauchery. Sodom and Gomorrah in Ontario. The nadir of our sad and sorry lives since we lost the Garden." My father, beside me, snoozes, probably dreaming of a roof he shingled the day before in the midday sun, or a speckled trout he caught under the bridge over Snake Creek where the water runs dark and cool. My mother is on the far side of my brother, too far away to inconspicuously wake him. My brother hands me a butterscotch candy. I wait until the Reverend whirls by, then I unwrap it slowly and sensuously, take my time placing it on my tongue. It melts in a prolonged welter of butter and beauty. This *migh*t be the taste of sin, I think. This might be *my* sin. If so, it's not bad at all.

Monarchs Softball Team, 1950. Roger holding ball,
his dad, Bob Bell, back row, second from left.

RADIO SILENCE

I plead and plead and plead with my mother but it's like begging a tree to step aside. There is no way I am going to be allowed to stay home this afternoon to watch the seventh game of the World Series, do I understand? School comes first. I keep trying. "It's not just *any* game, Mom, it's the *seventh*. The curse of the Bambino. Ace against ace. Bob Gibson is starting against Jim Lonborg." Those names mean nothing to her. She sits eating her egg salad sandwich, smoking between bites, dreaming of being childless. If I would just shut up and go back to school she could finish that Harlequin Romance she is on the last chapter of. "Oh, please?" I am almost in tears, quite undignified for an 18-year-old, but if tears will move her, I'll use them. A bite of sandwich, chew chew, a drag on the cigarette, a bite of icicle pickle, of sandwich, chew chew, another drag, a look of long suffering. "Nope."

I hammer every stair tread hard on the way up to my room, shit shit shit shit shit, say my boots, and I slam the door behind me. I have of late begun to see the world as unjust, particularly as it concerns me. How the hell can missing one afternoon's school be such a big deal? My marks are better than good, I'll be an Ontario Scholar, I'm on my way to university, I keep my nose clean—no dope busts, no pregnant girlfriends, no overturned cars. I deserve this baseball game.

My eyes light on my transistor radio, sitting quietly on the dresser. Next to that dresser is my briefcase. I put the brain my mother is so proud of to use. Two hours later my body's in Frisky Freddy's math class, with my head in Fenway. My desk is beside the windows that look out over the October-tinged trees and the playing field. It's warm for October, Series weather, the windows are open. My briefcase sits on the window side of my desk, in it my transistor radio, out of which runs the earpiece wire that snakes up under my shirt, along the sleeve, where it exits at the cuff. I am leaning on my left elbow, my hand cupping my head, the tiny plastic bud nestling inside my eager ear.

The first two innings are equal. Each team gets one on in the first, but both are stranded. My hero Roger Maris, ex-Yankee, he of 61 homers and 142 RBIs in 1961, singles, beating out a slow hopper to the mound, but Orlando Cepeda grounds out to end it. For the Sox, Joey Foy walks, gets sacrificed to second, but Yaz pops up and Bud Harrelson is fanned by Big Bob, who's throwing heat. In the Cards' second, with two out, Javier is walked but unwisely tries to steal second; Ellie Howard, another ex-Yank, guns him down. The Bosox second ends when Rico Petrocelli whiffs on a fastball high and tight.

The third decides things. Light-hitting Dal Maxvill triples to the gap in centre. But Gibson lines out and Lou Brock pops up. Then good old Curt Flood singles and Maxville speeds home. Lonborg, going on only two days' rest, begins to labour. Maris singles to right, Curt zips to third. Then Lonborg throws a wild pitch, Flood speeds home, Maris advances to second. And a hand firmly grasps my right shoulder. "Are you asleep?" asks Frisky Freddy. My head jerks towards him so fast I get whiplash, and the earbud pops out where it dangles conspicuously on my wrist. "Because I've asked you something three times and you haven't responded." I try to palm the earbud but he's spotted it. His face is hawk-like, his glasses sliding down his sharp nose. "What have we here?" Freddy has a nasty smile. I have seen him flash it on occasion, such as when he parted my friend's hair one day with a hurled piece of chalk. "Stand up, please." I do, and the radio tugs itself half out of the briefcase. "We *wouldn't*, by chance, or *design*, be tuned in to the World Series, *would* we?" The way he is italicizing certain words as he says them worries me.

"Yessir." "Who's winning?" "St. Louis, sir." "And the score? We want to know the score, *don't* we class?" "2-0, sir." His smile has vanished; he silently holds out his hand; I extricate the wire, turn it and the radio over to him, watch sullenly as he puts them in his desk drawer, and conspicuously locks it.

By the time that class is over, and the next, by the time I have sat meekly in Fast Freddy's room getting my ears chewed off and having him tell me that I'll be busy doing the extra hundred questions he's given me for the next day, by the time I have sprinted home and flicked on the TV, the game is in the bottom of the eighth, with Norm Siebern pinch-hitting for Santiago; there is a force at second, but Petrocelli scores. And that is the last run of the game, the Cards will win it 7-2, take the series. Bob Gibson will be the hero, a three-game winner. The weather turns that night; a big wind comes in, pushing cold air, about the time I am falling asleep over question 67.

I get up very early the next morning to work on math, spend my spare and all lunch on it, get it done in time for Frisky Freddy, who, with a smirk, hands me back my radio in front of the whole class. "I hope you got to watch at least some of the game." "Yessir, I did, thank you for asking," I reply as sugar-sweetly as possible, but what I am sourly imagining is Big Bob Gibson on the mound, leaning toward the plate, malice and intent dripping off that pure black face, Frisky Freddy quavering in the batter's box, nothing but a flimsy piece of white chalk in his hands, and then a hundred-mile-an-hour fastball humming like radio waves right at his self-satisfied head.

BATTLE SONG

It is a Sunday night, after dinner, there are hours of summer daylight left, I am wondering if I should go out on my tricycle, maybe see if Norma Lynn wants to ride on the back step while I pedal furiously, or play with the new kittens whose eyes are not yet open. There used to be five of them but now there are just four, since my little brother tossed one up in the air to prove to me that cats always land on their feet. It fell instead on its head with a thwap. He cried, gently cradled it and put it back in beside the mother, but it wouldn't move. Later, my dad took it and buried it among the phlox. My mom is washing the remaining dishes, my dad drying. With a flourish, he twirls the towel inside and around the last glass and puts it in its place, then he turns to me.

"Know what tonight is?" I shake my head. "Pipers," he grins, "at the beach. Want to go?" Yes, yes, of course I do, he knows that. The pipers, I *love* the pipers, he knows that. The snap snap snap of the snares, the POOM-POOM of the big bass drum, the kilts swirling, the pipes wailing. And we often march along, he and I, in military precision, arms keeping time. If I can't keep up he swings me into his arms and marches with me, saying, "This is how we marched in the war." Yes, I want to go to the beach. My mom says, "You can't go like that," wrings out the wet dishcloth and wipes the last of the chocolate cake off my face. The cloth smells of supper, of roast beef and mashed potatoes and carrots. I twist my head but she holds me firmly. She brushes my curly hair; my younger brother's she combs because it is so fine and blond. Then we all pile into the two-door green Pontiac, Jim and I in the back seat bouncing in anticipation. My father is singing:

> Upon the Lomonds I lay, I lay
> upon the Lomonds I lay, I lay, I lay,
> I lookit down to bonnie Lochleven
> and saw three perches play-hay-hay.

He drums upon the steering wheel as he sings. I like the sound of the word Lochleven. It has that little throat catch in the middle.

The beach is crowded, cars parked all over the place. And it is beginning to spit rain. "We will just stay in the car and listen," says my mom. I lean up between the front seats and look at my dad. He wants to be out there striding along beside the pipers, but he also knows not to argue with my mom. "We'll open the door," he says. "We can hear better that way and still stay dry." And he swings his big door open just as the band begins, the pipes swelling from a preliminary drone into their full voice, the drums joining them. It is our favourite song, *The Campbells Are Comin'*. "This is a battle march," says my dad, as his hands keep time and my feet start tapping. "The Campbells are comin', Ho-Ro, Ho-Ro!" sings my dad, and I join in. The band is going to march right by us. I feel my blood race and the hair stand up on the back of my neck. It is raining a bit harder now but my dad keeps the door open; I lean out between the seat back and the door post see better.

> The great Argyll he goes before,
> he makes the cannons and guns to roar,
> with sound o' trumpet, pipe and drum,
> the Campbells are comin', Ho-Ro, Ho-Ro!

My dad sings like I have never heard him do, that big loose grin I love plastered on his face. He exaggerates his Rs, holding them and rrrrrolling them off his tongue. The car is rocking with our Ro-Ho-ing. I believe I can hear *cannons and guns to roar*, but my mom says, "Bob, that's thunder." My mom is afraid of thunder and lightning; when it really storms her eyes roll back in her head like an animal's and she tucks herself into corners. And the rain is getting harder, though the band continues. She pleads with my dad to close the door. I have time to pull back my head, but not my hand. The door closes with a solid thwump, and the sound of the pipes is cut off. The car is silent for a long moment, there is strange distance, then my hand begins to scream, I begin to echo that scream, my dad turns, wondering, my mom sees what is wrong, yells at him to "open back up, open the goddam door, Bob, his hand is in it!" The big grin slides from his face as he swings it open, stumbles out to help me, tips the seat forward, sweeps me up into his strong arms. All the way up the street our car is like a police car, my voice the siren.

Before I know it, I am sitting up on the kitchen counter, my hand plunged into a bowl of ice water, my tears slowing. My dad musses my hair and whispers into my ear, "Enough tears now, enough, you're a Scot, and Scots are tough. "

"Am I the Great Argyll?" I sniffle. "Greater," he says. "Tough as nails," he adds. I flex my fingers; nothing seems broken. By the next morning I have moved past it. My hand is stiff, but it works. The following weekend another pipe band comes to town; and it is raining again. My mom and brother stay in the car, but my dad tells her that there'll be no cars for us this week. If the pipers can march in the rain, so can we. With banners a rattlin' in the wind, my dad and I march, our arms swinging to the beat of our blood.

BLIND MAN'S BUFF

Fred sits in the big arm chair in the curtain-dimmed living room with his head held erect, listening intently. He has his arms flat upon the arms of the overstuffed chair, formally; I have seen pictures of ancient kings sitting thus. Fred is blind, has two glass eyes that he will remove upon request, though it sickens me to see him do so. "I take them out at night," he tells us as we listen raptly, "and put them on the bedside table. They watch as I sleep, keep vigil for me. No one can sneak up on me, no one, not even Death." I can imagine those eyes, their unbending stare; what I can't imagine is how they warn Fred if danger approaches. Do they roll together with a clack, the way marbles do as we play with them at school?

Right now he is very still, seems frozen in place. Jim and I are sneaking closer, our shoes and socks removed for ultimate stealth. I bend my foot down toe to heel, the way Indians do in films, the way we were taught in Cub Scouts. I can hear Great Aunt Lizzie rolling out pie crust on the kitchen table, a *garumph* each time the wooden cylinder elongates the dough. Great Uncle Charlie is sitting on the side veranda reading the newspaper, and the pages riffle in the wind. In here is only the sound of our breathing and the occasional groan from the wide wooden floor boards giving way under us. We have learned where they are, try to avoid them, but they are treacherous. Fred says they are his sentries. In this version of Blind Man's Buff the blinded one is static; the goal is to touch Fred on the knee before he spots us, before he lifts his cane, points it right at one of us and says, "There." Then you are out. Then the other must go it alone. If one of us succeeds, he will hand us his tin of humbugs and we may take one.

The cane dangles down the chair front from the finger tips of his right hand. I watch it warily as I get closer and closer. Neither of us has ever buffed the blind man, that's how astute he is. Aunt Lizzie says his ears have taken over for his eyes, that he can hear a bull bellow from my Uncle Walker's farm way across the river. His world is reduced to sound and touch now, she says, and he is sharp. Sometimes he follows us with his head, like radar, but today he is a sphinx. Jim is behind his chair and I approach from the front left; our strategy is to confuse him by dividing his attention. I have learned to watch the cane, watch for the slightest movement. I believe I have him, finally, I am that close. By the time he gets the cane up I'll have tapped his left knee. I begin to smile as my arm lifts towards him. I have suspended my breathing; there is nothing for him to hear but Aunt Lizzie's rolling pin and Uncle Charlie's paper flapping. I watch the cane, reach out, watch the cane, and don't see his left hand shoot out to grab my arm, but I feel its electricity and I jump so hard I bite my tongue as he stands and yells simultaneous with his grab, "Gotcha!"

I'm sucking blood and my heart is trip-hammering a hole in my chest and Fred is laughing to beat the band. Jim takes this opportunity to finish his approach, home free, he thinks, *home free*, when Fred lets my arm drop, spins on his heel, stabs the cane at my brother, who is amazed and paralyzed where he stands. "There," Fred roars, and we both hang our heads. The blind man laughs and laughs and laughs, then gets control of himself. He sits down, takes a tin from his pocket, twists off the lid and offers it to us. "You almost had me today, boys," he says, as we each take a mint, unwrap it, pop it in our mouths and start sucking. "Maybe someday soon...In the meantime, you deserve a reward." But we know we will never beat him.

Soon after, he takes ill, is hospitalized. "Poor thing," says Aunt Lizzie, "he won't ever get out." My dad takes me up to see him. We enter his room and see the old man stretched out in bed; he appears to be sleeping. On the table beside him, in a water-filled container, sit his eyes. *Keeping vigil.* I move towards the bed, watching the eyes in the glass watch me. "Fred?" My dad touches my shoulder. "Don't wake him," he says. I ignore him, continue silently towards Fred, reach out to touch the sheets that cover him. I am not sure he is breathing. Until an arm shoots out from beneath the sheets and seizes me. "Still gotcha," says Fred, chuckles painfully, then subsides, his hand gently releasing me, and he says no more.

Market Street tricycle and wagon gang, circa 1954.
Roger 4th from left, in helmet, behind Jim.

TWO WHEELS

I have waited for this for so long - to be a bigger boy. A tricycle is for little boys who wear short pants, it has three wheels, is solid and safe, a neighbourhood conveyance. But two wheels adds risk and reward both, two wheels fledges you, puts the whole town and more at your disposal.

My dad comes walking home from work today wheeling a bike, guiding it with one hand, his tool box in the other. He grins when he sees me. I abandon what I'm doing on the side porch with my cat and her newest batch of kittens in a cardboard box. "Mine?" I ask, afraid he might say no, he's just found it at the corner, he'll call the police and have them come get it. "Yours." He sets down the tool box and lifts me up onto the seat. He smells of sunshine and sweat and sawdust. It is cherry red with white fenders. Not new, but that means nothing as I lean onto the handlebars and clumsily try the pedals. A foreign land, this machine, high up, unstable. He puts a strong, brown hand on the left bar beside mine, his right behind me on the seat, and begins to walk me around the yard, out to the alley, back to the porch.

My mom comes out, a bowl of something she's stirring in her hands. "Isn't it a bit big for him?" she asks. My mom worries about things, he must know I'm afraid she'll veto it until I am older. "He's ready," he tells her firmly, "and if it's a bit too big, he'll grow into it. He's past the tricycle stage." The hand he has wrapped around mine on the left grip gives a reassuring squeeze. My mom shakes her head, turns, still stirring but harder now, fingers white on the spoon, steps back into her kitchen where no one disagrees with her, the door slapping behind her disapprovingly. He lifts me down, leans the bike against the porch. I don't want off yet. He reads my mind. "After supper," he says, stroking the back of the mother cat and picking up one of the mewling babies to see if its eyes are open yet, "I'll teach you how to ride it."

I hardly eat. My mom is the world's best cook but her lettuce salad with cream and brown sugar dressing and her new potatoes in butter and her steak braised in the oven hold no allure. The first thing I'll do is turn the handlebars around and up, like a bull's horns. I'll attach a baseball card to the rear frame so it snaps against the spokes. I'll get a headlight and maybe a carrier, a job delivering papers or groceries. Dad eats slowly and appreciatively. He eats two pieces of pie, has a third cup of coffee. I am dying more with each forkful, each sip. He sets his empty mug on the table, leans his chair back, pats his stomach appreciatively. "That was great," he says to my mom, who glows with his praise. She lives to feed us. "You okay with the dishes?" he asks her; he likes to dry while she washes, they'll talk quietly around suds and hot water, sometimes he'll slide his hand around her waist and pull her to him, kiss her neck, he'll say, "How about a cuddle?" She'll laugh and shove him away, maybe give him a face wash with the dishrag. "Get out of here, both of you," she says. I jump up, run out, my dad behind me. As the screen door shuts, I hear her parting doubt: "And for God's sake, be careful."

He shows me how to get on as he holds the bike upright for me – hands on the bars, left foot heavy into the left pedal, right leg swings over the bar and left foot lands on its pedal. Step down step down step down, and we begin to move. He jogs along beside me, keeps me steady, little pressures here and there. Guiding. Steadying. Around and around the house we go. He stops, catches his breath. "Time for concrete," he says. We leave the yard and head over to the parking lot of Charlie Schell's service station. Ten minutes later we stop. "You have it," he says, "time for me to start letting go." I get tight all over. I feel like I will pitch sideways. "Not completely, don't worry, just a few seconds at a time. I will be right beside you, just touching the seat."

And it works. Back and forth, the sun getting lower, along past the church, past the gravestone place, turn, do the block again. As I pass in front of the church, I look down at the stretched shadow behind and to the left, boy on a bike and his dad connected just there. I check again a few revolutions further on, see boy on a bike and *no one just there!* Way back and there he is, at the corner grinning. The bars lurch left as if malevolently grabbed by an unseen hand and the wheel goes perpendicular to my path and I am launched. I fly for a short time, then slam to the sidewalk, in this order: knees, elbows, chin.

My mother, who is sitting placidly on the side porch knitting, shrieks when we round the corner, drops the ball of yarn and the needles, runs to us, my dad carrying me under one arm, the bike under the other. Where he carries me his work shirt is covered in snot and tears and blood. He is no longer grinning, and what my mother says to him sets his mouth into a grim slit. She plucks me from his arms and tears into the house with me. For the next half hour she swabs at my shredded knees and elbows, dabs at my chin, gets as much gravel as possible out. Then she smears the wounds with cow salve ("good for man or beast" it says on the tin) and covers them with gauze and white tape. She makes me whipped jello, lets me eat the whole bowl, gently brushes my curly hair, then she tucks me into bed beside my brother and I blubber for a long time, like a big baby, until I start to get drowsy and my weeping ceases.

I can hear Mom's voice downstairs, still raised. I can't hear it all but "...told you he wasn't big enough yet," drifts up. "You're wrong," I say aloud but she will never hear me over her excoriation of my dad. There'll be no cuddling there tonight.

The next morning my arms and legs scream as I get out of bed. The stairs are a test. I feel like Frankenstein's monster, all stiff limbed, herky-jerky. My dad is already gone to work. Mom hugs me, gets me breakfast, then sets me on the counter and unceremoniously rips the tape and gauze off me. "Time to let some air at those," she pronounces. I should cry but I think I left all my tears in bed last night. I go outside. The bike is still leaning where my dad left it last night as he tried to evade my mom's tongue-lashing. I look at my knees; that clear stuff is still seeping out. I bend my legs, tentatively, then my arms. They still work. I stand the bike up, grip the bars, left foot down, right leg over, *owwwww*, right foot down. And fall over. I start to groan, muffle it. If she hears me, my mom will be out here in a flash. I get up, again try the mount. Step down. Step down, step down, step down.

And I am moving, wobbling slightly but moving. *On. My. Own.* I leave the yard. I should tell Mom, but why get that trouble going. When she looks for me, sees the bike gone, she'll know. She'll worry, but when doesn't she? The further I go the less I wobble. My knees protest, but not unbearably so. I know where my dad is working, I head there, pumping. And there he is, one knee steadying a piece of wood laid across two sawhorses, muscular arm ripping a saw blade through a piece of spruce, push, pull, push. I yell, he stops, wipes the sweat from his eyes. I wave, he grins broadly, waves back. I pass him, slow and circle, pass him again. He leans the saw against the sawhorse, applauds. On my next pass he is back at the wood, just lifts his head to nod, once, then looks back down at his work, intent upon the saw teeth biting along the line he has drawn.

I do not stop beside him, indeed am afraid to stop, now that I am moving. I am in synch with the machine and gravity. Down to the lake I go, back up and out east to the Mill Creek Bridge, over past the dump and the cemetery, out to the tobacco fields, back to the main corner. I slow as I approach it. Where to now? I teeter for a moment, almost panic, then steady myself. Anywhere I want.

Roger, 1967, very cool baby blue mohair sweater.

IT BEGINS TO END

I am on a train, stretched out in a narrow upper bunk, trying to sleep, but though it is well past midnight my body is humming like a struck tuning fork and I know it will be hours before I drop off. Outside a Northern Ontario I can't see is blurring by. We are on our way west, to the Pacific. I have never been out of Ontario, except for when I was small, a trip to the Buffalo Zoo with my Fort Erie cousins, and my dad held me out over the alligators until I screamed and my Mom made him set me down.

Four hours ago, before he saw me off at Union Station, my dad took me to Maple Leaf Gardens to see my first NHL game live. The place was electric with noise and anticipation. No idea how many games I had watched on TV Saturday nights with my family. But to be in this shrine and see these players as *real,* feel the cold air swish up to us as they rushed by. Bobby Orr, the sensational rookie for the Bruins, ten months older than I, was on the ice with these legends. The moment came when Orr paused with the puck behind his own net, calming it, claiming it, then slowly began the up-ice journey, gaining speed, accelerating more, swooping elegantly and deking, and never passing, never using his teammates except as decoys, never once being touched by a Leaf, all of them waving in vain as he swept past them, alone and in control, that magnificent kid, end to end, and tucking the puck high past the sprawling goalie, so that even that Leaf crowd, home team lovers all, had to rise to their feet and applaud.

Then my dad was handing me my suitcase somewhere in the cavernous bowels of the station while a train steamed impatiently and my classmates and I piled nervously on. We settled in, and the train moved, shuffling slowly at first, then hurtling headlong into the night.

Then morning. Snow and trees and rocks and lakes, and that again and that again and nothing much else, so we begin playing marathon euchre, shuffling, dealing, trumping, looking out occasionally to see movement but no change. Clubs, rocks, Spades, lakes, Hearts, snow, Diamonds, trees. Meals and movement. And bed. And by the next morning something different. Winnipeg rising into being for two hours, so some bored brave fools exit against the rules to explore and are almost left behind. Then flatter land than I have ever seen, and speed. Saskatoon, a thirty-minute stop, a teacher jumps off into the arms of her family, we didn't even know she was from somewhere else, then gone again, goodbye, goodbye. She is crying. We avert our eyes, grant her what privacy we can, watch the Prairies flash by. Think of our own families, farther away than they have ever been.

Sleep again, now used to being rocked to the rhythm of the train. And we awake to rising foothills, then... Our mouths hang open, we feel dwarfed. South of our town Highway 21 goes up over what we locals call the Mountain. I feel a foolish rube, to have ever called it that. I swear to myself I never will again. Our *Mountain* is just a hill, not even a big one, miniscule beside these rugged things that tower above us as we follow swift rivers, hugging the sheer sides of rock cuts. Out the riverside windows you can see train cars that have derailed and lie twisted and abandoned far below. Every time the train sways, you feel death, like a troll, waiting.

Then the Okanagan, oh sweet valley, where the air is spring warm and redolent of flowers and crop growth. The conductor lets us take turns standing in small groups on the back porch of the caboose, in our shirt sleeves. We are winter-bruised, we breathe, deeply. Then more mountains and we descend into Vancouver. Salt-smell. For most of us, it is our first ocean. Still snow in Ontario, but here is green grass and daffodils. At my first breakfast there I ask for salmon, and the waitress, who has red hair and really nice breasts, smiles at me and says, "That is an unusual request, young man," and I say "Well, I have never had fresh Pacific salmon before, and I'm only here for three days and then it's back to tinned salmon" and she says, "In that case..." At nine in the morning somewhere in a city of hills and water I am savouring fine red-fleshed fish and golden fries and crunch creamy coleslaw while around me the unadventurous are slobbering down greasy bacon and smeared eggs sopped up with toast that their moms will cook them every day of the week back home.

Seventy two hours later we are headed back east, one hundred and forty-four hours later we are back in our desks in school. *What just happened?* I ask myself. On the train my partner and I played over 900 games of euchre and won over 700. After our last game, near Sudbury, she leaned over and kissed me on the cheek, said, "We'd make a good team." I blushed, I caught what I thought might be a proposal I wasn't ready for, I stammered something stupid and non-committal. During the trip the younger sister of a teacher cleaned out a big farm boy with a fat wallet. She snuggled up to him from the Okanagan in, hung on him like fog on a mountaintop all over Vancouver while he bought her clothes and good meals and even tinned fresh air from the top of Grouse Mountain, then she spurned him the minute his funds faltered our last night there and took up with another guy whom she told she'd always loved. I caught a nasty cold and honked and snorfled for the whole trip home. On our last night aboard the train I got up to pee and saw the chaperone father of one student, reeking of rye, crawl out of the curtained bunk of the mother of another student. He stopped when he saw me, smiled, put his finger to his lips in the shhhh sign, tipped an imaginary hat to me, and wobbled back to his bunk.

After school, I drive out to the Mountain. I feel sorry for it, I wish it could live up to how I used to see it, instead of diminished. I U-turn, head back to town, never once looking in my rear-view mirror.

ALL YOUNG PEOPLE SHOULD TRAVEL

It is midnight, and four of us are packed into my friend's Acadian Beaumont, rolling through the summer-lush farm country. We are headed towards Montreal, and Expo '67, because it is Centennial Year, and because Pierre Trudeau has said all young people should travel and see their country.

Our last day of high school is behind us. It was anti-climactic - a few awkward hugs and handshakes, a lot of false bravado. We'll see one another at graduation in the fall anyway. By then some will be working for their dads the way it was ordained they'd be from the time they were born; others will be in university, either happily loading up on hallucinogens and skipping class and having afternoon sex in a haze of hemp smoke, or sadly studying alone in libraries until midnight. A few will head to Europe or Yorkville or the early oblivion of marriage and kids.

We had our prom. Our theme was the South Seas, with a volcano that was supposed to bubble lava but just made wet, farting sounds. I took a girl from Underwood, our first date though I had known her for three years. My hand shook violently as I tried to pin on her corsage, because I was touching her amazingly warm, soft breast and her mom and dad were standing vigilantly nearby. After the dance we went to some guy's place near the school and she and I drank a bottle of warm sparkling wine, then some not much colder beer, then rye. We tried to neck on the sagging couch but our coordination was bad by then, so somebody drove us out to her place. She fell getting out of the car but I gallantly hoisted her up and got her to the door, where she amazed me with a kiss so sensual and profound I was still standing there swaying five minutes after she'd gone in and shut out the lights her parents had left on for her.

I think about her now as we drive, I wonder if that kiss was the end or the beginning. The windows are all down, the soft night pushing in, the radio is on and the driver and I are singing along with Jim, *C'mon baby, light my fire.* Which morphs into Lulu and her aching *To Sir with Love,* and that into Van the Man's bouncy *Brown-eyed Girl.* The radio will change only as stations slip away - Tommy James and the Shondells' overtly sexual *I Think We're Alone Now* becomes static - and new ones are tuned in - Bobby Gentry wails that *Billy Joe McAllister jumped offa Tallahachee Bridge.* There is almost no other traffic and the car moves unimpeded towards where the world has built a welcome on an island in the St. Lawrence.

The sun rises over Quebec as we cross the border and we have breakfast in a Greek restaurant in Montreal. None of us has ever been to this province before and we wonder if the French that Cecil Wright painstakingly taught us for five years of high school will get us through. Turns out we are staying in the basement of a monastery owned by les Frères de Sacre Coeur, and they speak English, and that a whole bunch of guys our age from Ohio are staying, and their English is hard to decipher. Turns out you can buy quarts of beer in Montreal, and you can get it in the corner stores, and that before the end of the first day we and the Americans are plastered, one of them so badly so that he almost stops breathing and we send him by ambulance to hospital and a Brother comes down to chide us for our intemperance; he is fat but kind, and I am reminded of the Friar in *Romeo and Juliet.* And like Romeo, I ignore his advice.

We spend long hours, often standing in interminable lines, at the Exposition. My stomach lurches through North of Superior in the Cinesphere, which is a theatre vastly superior to the one in Southampton we all go to twice a week. I see pavilion after pavilion until they begin to run together. Then in the Austrian Pavilion I meet a tall brunette hostess, we talk a bit, she agrees even though she is taller than I am and she is twenty and I am eighteen, and she speaks five languages and I speak two, sort of, to meet at ten o'clock tonight for drinks. I tell my friends and they laugh at me, say she's jerking my chain, ten will come, then eleven, and I will be waiting. *They are right*, I think, when ten arrives, the wind has risen off the river and it's getting chilly, the crowds have thinned to just the stragglers, *I am a chump.* Then she is beside me, takes me by the arm, leads me to a late hours beer garden and we sit and talk about who we are and what our lives are like. How sophisticated she is, how European, how many things she has seen, places she has been. And how parochial I am. But she can't hear enough about life in Bruce County, Ontario, Canada. And the way she laughs and leans across the table and covers my hand with hers, oh. It gets very late; she seems to genuinely regret what she has to say, that our time is over. She won't let me walk her home. She holds my hands. "You are a good boy, a genuine person," she says in her slightly clipped English. I don't want her to call me *boy*, don't want her to go, know I am powerless to prevent any of it. She leans over and places on my lips a kiss that holds warmth and womanliness and worldliness, but no promise. She smiles then, turns, disappears, her heels clacking. I walk alone back across the whole high shivering Jacques Cartier Bridge, that huge lonely river below powering its inexorable way to the unseen ocean. I wearily come to where my friends have fallen into a beery sleep and the Sacred Heart watches protectively over them, as if they are naïfs who are lost in a new land.

GIVING WAY

June has given way to July; the year is coming to fruition. I find myself sprawled with a young woman across the front seat of my parents' Pontiac. She is here for the summer working in a lodge, staying with other girls all from somewhere else. Girls from farther away have a cachet for town boys, and they have no parents to wait up for them, to stare hard at you when you get them home at 3 a.m. We met a day after I got back from Expo and since then we have been *seeing each other.* And tonight I am seeing more of her than I ever have of any female. We're in a tangle of clothes in a steamed-up Pontiac Strato-Chief, and the breeze off the nearby lake would be a mercy, but parked where we are, up in a grove of cedars at the end of a cottage road, rolling down the windows would expose us to a million mosquitoes more savage than the heat.

"Was I okay?" she murmurs into my ear, and I answer, "Wonderful," though I am lying, I have no idea how she was, having no standard with which to compare. I can't tell her I was a virgin until fifteen minutes ago, though I know she wasn't. Her boyfriend from last summer told me she'd put out for him. I don't ask her how I was. I can guess. It was fast and fumbly, it was messy, that I know. I feel spent, and at peace. And a little embarrassed.

We disentangle, shrug back into our clothes, I turn on the radio, she leans across the seat, puts her head on my shoulder, my arm slides around her shoulders. We back out into the world and roll down the windows on the shore road, letting the lake air wick away our sweat.

Then we go to the Lido Café, sit on the vinyl seats of a booth across from each other. It is late, there are many drunks from the beverage room in there. Some of our friends, too, but we don't invite them to join us. We order chips and gravy and Cokes. When the food comes, we twirl our forks in the glutinous mess and shove greasy wads of it into our mouths, as if we haven't eaten in years. We gulp the icy Cokes and ask for re-fills. Sex is thirsty work. The green fluorescent lights don't do anything for her; I suspect I look no better. Her clothes are wrinkled, her hair tangled, her makeup smeared. We might as well have what we just did written on our foreheads.

I take her back to the darkened lodge, walk her to the foot of the stairs that lead to the top floor. She has to be up to serve breakfast in five hours, and I have to be out suckering tobacco plants. We kiss wearily, she goes in, I go home, tread carefully past my mother dozing on the couch. I won't wake her; I'm afraid what she might read in my face. I strip, shower, dry off, fall into bed, sleep the sleep of the dead.

WITH A LONG SIGH

With a long sigh, summer relinquishes its hold. The days become bittersweet, a desperate attempt to hold onto something that won't be held. Stores put their beach wares on sale, the not yet selected shovels and pails, air mattresses, bathing suits calling out to passersby like birds left behind by a migrating flock. A few cottages are shuttered and left early, the number of tourists gently declines. All slides inexorably towards Labour Day Weekend, that bend in the road around which lies, unofficially but realistically, fall.

And then it's there, though it can't be, the sun is too high and benevolent, the water at the beach still too warm to abandon, and sparkling seductively. But it is Monday and the exodus has begun; by late afternoon the highway south is car after groaning car, loaded with a season, with kids and dogs and their sad faces hanging out windows taking one last look until next year. They cannot wait until evening to depart; new clothes to be tried on and notebooks to sign and lunches to be packed for school wait. We are sitting on a bench in front of the bank, as we do every year on this day, watching the ebbing of the tide. The girl from the lodge is gone. We lasted only another two weeks after our night in the cedars. She and I never did fall in love. The girl from Hamilton I did fall insanely in love with soon after is back home in Hamilton, three hours away; I will phone her after supper tonight, tell her how the town emptied, how most of the cottages are now closed until next May 24th, and those that aren't will be on Thanksgiving, that a whole part of the town has been put to bed early. She'll find it hard to believe, knowing the town as summer-vital, always leaving before it diminishes.

Monday night at the roller rink it's all locals. The music echoes unnaturally in the almost empty space. Last night it was packed with bodies whirling counter-clockwise around an oval to throbbing music; tonight we are trying to fill it and failing so we mostly stand around talking softly, our lame conversations like the back roads around here that start as paved, then go to gravel, then dirt, then just peter out as if they forgot where they were going. Some skaters, like my brothers, will be back in school tomorrow. Some of us, those *heading off*, will be in limbo another two weeks, an unfamiliar mid-place for us; we will be neither here nor there.

I keep working on tobacco, it's harvest and the rush is on to beat the frosts we know are coming. The long days of toil fill both kilns and our bank accounts. Then that morning comes when we load my stuff in a car and drive south to university. I look out the back window until we have crested the Mountain and the highway drops down the other side. I can't see my town any more, so I draw my eyes inward and wonder about the *there* I'm aiming at. I sense it's bigger. I know next May I will come back, only like a tourist this time, here but with some of me residing elsewhere. Things will have changed without me. Except for the lake. The lake will still be there, it always is, it never disappoints.

W H A T DO YOU KNOW?

What do you know, anyway? Well, you know your phone number, obviously, 66W, and that of your best friend, 249J. Each has three or four digits, the last of which is a letter. You pick the receiver up out of its cradle, the voice of a woman who is sitting in the office just west of the bank comes on and asks you, "What number, please?" You tell her, she says "One moment, please," (she is so unfailingly polite) and you are connected.

You know where your cat is buried. Where to get the watercress your mother loves in between slices of buttered bread, where to get the morels your dad fries in the big iron frying pan. Your grandparents' mailbox is number 14. You get their mail for them every day. The Toronto Telegram that you pick up each day at Cluley's, on the way back from the Post Office, is number 7, written in blue crayon at the top. You cut your grandparents' lawn for them Thursday afternoons, and you know to do the edges with the non-motorized reel mower and the rest with the motorized reel mower. You know that the grass that accumulates in the grass catcher goes in the sack and the sack is tied with a piece of binder twine and that the garbage men will, each week, untie that sack, dump the clippings into the back of the truck, then fold up the sack with the twine coiled on top and leave it beneath the maple tree. You know not to dive off the playground side of the break-wall, or you'll snap your neck on the sandy bottom. It's much deeper on the outer side, but remember to push out past the rocks. You know that when the wind is onshore the water may be bathtub warm but that if the wind shifts to offshore, it becomes cold enough to make your teeth ache and your testicles clench. You know foot-long hotdogs are better at the Tuck Shop and that french fries are better at the Town Booth. You know Charlie Drummond at the Sunoco gas station will give you more ice cream than you can get at the Dairy Bar for the same money, if you don't mind a bit of grease on the cone or cigar ash on the top scoop. You know that the girls up the street pee in their grandmother's rain barrel, then laugh secretly as she washes her hair with the soft water.

You know who lives where. The witch lives in the house with the long grass and the sagging porch, the one you fell through delivering her paper. The only cop in town lives near the library, where his wife works. The candy store man and his sick wife live behind the candy store. The hardware store family live above the hardware store. The butcher and his wife and daughters dwell a storey above his sawdust-covered cutting-room floor, very sharp knives and carnal display cases. The family who make french fries and runs the dance hall live beside the Presbyterian manse. The elementary school janitor lives just west of you, the high school janitor just south, near the bicycle repair man.

One thing you don't really know, or care to know, is most street names. The main street is called Goderich, but it is always "uptown" or "downtown." You don't ever say, "I'm going to Goderich Street." because that would be considered stupid. Although it *is* logically named: if you follow Goderich Street south and don't stop in Amberly for ice-cream, in an hour you will get to Goderich. The street you live on is Waterloo, the one where you used to live, Market. You know the streets that run to the lake, from north to south perpendicular to Goderich they are: Market; Elgin; Mill, Green, Gustavus (well, it goes to the fairgrounds, as does Johnson next to it, but you can get to the lake through the fairgrounds. The lake is what counts here. Everyone wants to go to the lake. It is the defining feature.) Aside from those few you don't know street names, nor do you need to. If you want to go to someone's house, you go. You don't stop first and think, I will go to Ken's house on Mill Street. Your brain is one big instinct-coloured map, bearing no letters, no numbers. There is almost no one in this place you don't know, but if that occurs, when someone is trying to tell you how to get to that house to deliver a newspaper or some groceries, that person will not say, "Go up Gustavus, turn left on Bricker, find number 22." Some houses don't even have numbers. Who needs them? That person will just say, "It's the house between the church and Horie Parker's, the one with the blue '57 Buick," and you'll know where to go.

The only time you feel lost is if some tourist stops you. "Excuse me, do you live here?" "Yes, all my life." "Great. Maybe you can help me. I'm trying to get to a friend's cottage on Shady Lane." You stare blankly. The tourist thinks, "Local yokel. Too much inbreeding." "Sorry," you say, "I don't know that street. But it must be near the lake." You point hopefully west. He can't believe you live in a town of less than 2000 and don't know the streets. "He said to turn off Ryder Road." Again, you shrug doltishly. Thinking you're playing him because he is a *tourass*, he turns red, slams back into his car, drives furiously off.

Ah well, you think, you might as well go to Murray's, play table-top hockey, listen to the Dave Clark Five. Murray lives above the bank. There are twenty eight steps up to his apartment. His grandmother, Mrs. Murray, after whom he was named, bakes the best coffee cake you have ever tasted. His mother knitted you a blue wool sweater. He moved here from Tillsonburg at the beginning of Grade Four. His favourite hockey team is the Detroit Red Wings, his favourite player Alex Delvecchio. His dad is from Lucknow and once drank too much elderberry wine at a neighbour's farm, and on the way home rolled his Model A Ford off the gravel road into a deep ditch. They have a push-button transmission Studebaker. Murray beat you at golf yesterday, shooting 38 to your 43. You triple-bogeyed hole number five. You have only ever parred that hole three times in your life. He is six-feet and one half inch tall. You are five-five. In Grade Eight you were both five-four. The 45 rpm record of the Dave Clark Five has *Glad All Over* on the A side. The B is *I Know You.* You know everything you need to know. The rest isn't worth the bother.

Roger Bell grew up in Port Elgin, Ontario, on the shores of Lake Huron. He taught secondary school English in Midland and Penetanguishene for 29 years and lives in Tay Township, within dreaming distance of Georgian Bay.

He was a three-time finalist in the CBC/Tilden/Saturday Night competition, and a finalist for the People's Poetry Award and the 2011 Winston Collins/Descant Poem of the Year Award. In 1997, he was the first winner of the Shaunt Basmajian Chapbook Contest for his book Luke and the Wolf. He won the 2008 Cyclamens and Swords Poetry Competition. He has published six books of poetry, most recently You Tell Me (2009). His work has been read on the CBC and on National Public Radio in the US.

Bell is as storyteller who uses his poetry to write narratives about real life. His lyrical style is reminiscent of that of Canadian poet Al Purdy. He says his "goal as writer is to find the extraordinary within the ordinary."